Hilary
Th

υ

Roger Brown

The Conservative Counter-Revolution in Britain and America 1980–2020

palgrave
macmillan

Roger Brown
Solent University
Southampton, UK

ISBN 978-3-031-09141-4   ISBN 978-3-031-09142-1 (eBook)
https://doi.org/10.1007/978-3-031-09142-1

This Palgrave Macmillan imprint is published by the registered company Springer Nature Switzerland AG.
The registered company address is: Gewerbestrasse 11, 6330 Cham, Switzerland

PREFACE

This book is the product of nearly 40 years' thinking about higher education policy, inequality and social justice, macroeconomics and Neoliberalism, all of which come under the heading of what used to be called 'political economy'.

The book builds on some of my previous published work (listed in the References) as well as a number of unpublished papers. It started when I became interested in what was really driving the higher education reforms that I was variously devising, implementing, challenging and subverting between 1987 and 2017. With quite a strong progressive perspective, and unlike the Government, I was particularly concerned about the distributional consequences of these changes, especially for newer and less favoured institutions like Solent University and Liverpool Hope University (and their students), as well as the University of West London (where I served as an Independent Governor for several years).

This led me to inquire into and write about inequality: surely, the greatest challenge, after climate change, that our prosperous Western societies now face. This in turn led me to explore the part that Neoliberal policies of underfunding and privatisation have played in destroying or compromising so many aspects of our once highly regarded public realm: not only the universities but also the BBC, the NHS, the Civil Service, local government, social services, the arts (take your pick). I have now come to the conclusion that Neoliberalism, or at least Neoliberal theory, has really been used as a device to safeguard the interests of an economic elite and keep the mass of people in their place, and this is indeed the central argument of the book.

I should like to thank friends who willingly read and critiqued drafts: Bernard Abramson, Vaneeta D'Andrea, Tony Bruce, Helen Carasso, Jeff Richards and Richard Upson. My longstanding researcher Lilian Winkvist-Woods has once again provided invaluable assistance. Once again, too, I am indebted to the librarians at Solent University and Barton Peveril Sixth Form College Eastleigh for their help in finding and getting material. Finally, and above all, I am grateful to my lovely wife, Josie, for putting up with me while I was working on the book.

ACKNOWLEDGEMENT

The author wishes to gratefully acknowledge the permission given by University of Bristol Press for allowing him to use in Chap. 3 the quotation from *The Inequality Crisis: What Are the Facts and What We Can Do About It* (Policy Press 2017).

CONTENTS

CHAPTER 1

What This Book Is About

Abstract This chapter introduces the main argument of the book and explains how it is organised.

Keywords Conservative Party • Democracy • Monetarism • Neoliberalism • Populism • Republican Party

> *The conditions that neoliberalism demands in order to free human beings from the slavery of the state—minimal taxes, the dismantling of public services and social security, deregulation, the breaking of the unions—just happen to be the conditions to make the rich even richer, while leaving everyone else to sink or swim* (Monbiot, *2016*: 217–8). *What brought about this revolution was a successful intellectual and political movement, which used a set of ideas to take advantage of these crises* (Konczal, *2021*: 138).

In November 1984, at the age of 90, the former Prime Minister, the Earl of Stockton (previously, Mr. Harold Macmillan), made his maiden speech in the House of Lords. Besides warning—somewhat presciently, in view of the Johnson Government's 'levelling up' policy[1]—of a 'growing division of comparative prosperity in the south and an ailing north and Midlands', he asked where the theories of Monetarism had really come from:

> *"Was it America?" he inquired, "Or was it Tibet? It is quite true, many of your Lordships will remember it operating in the nursery. How do you treat a cold?" One nanny said, "Feed a cold"; she was a neo-Keynesian. The other said "Starve a cold"; she was a monetarist.* (Apple, 1984)

For some 30 years from the end of the World War II, the advanced economies of the West enjoyed an unprecedented period of prosperity. There were big increases in growth and productivity; there was full or near-full employment; inequality and poverty fell; home ownership increased; there was a considerable degree of financial stability. But since the late 1970s there have been much smaller increases in growth, productivity and investment; lower savings and higher debt (state, corporate and household); higher unemployment (with many leaving the labour market altogether); greater inequality and poverty; falling social mobility; increased fraud and other forms of crime; reduced trust, especially in institutions; and recurrent financial crises. Even the growth in home ownership has tailed off. Only on inflation has the performance of the major Western economies, since the late 1970s, been better than in the period since 1945, and even this has lately begun to change. Why did many Western countries—particularly the major Anglophone economies—abandon or move away from what on most economic and social criteria was a successful model of shared prosperity and security in favour of one that has so far been much less successful?[2]

The conventional explanation for what David Harvey (2005: 9) called the Neoliberal Turn is that the oil price rises of the early and mid-1970s led to rampant inflation and lower growth ('stagflation') which the interventionist Keynesian economic policies previously favoured failed to deal with. Instead, governments placed a new emphasis on monetary and fiscal discipline. This was reflected in the speech of one of Macmillan's successors (James Callaghan) to the 1976 Labour Party Conference:

> *We used to think that you could spend your way out of a recession and increase employment by cutting taxes and boosting government spending. I tell you in all candour that that option no longer exists, and in so far as it ever did exist, it only worked on each occasion since the war by injecting a bigger dose of*

inflation into the economy, followed by a higher level of unemployment as the next step. (BBC News Channel, 2005)

The triumph of the market was rendered complete by the implosion of the USSR and the collapse of Communism in the West in 1989–91.[3]

The central argument of this book is that the Neoliberal Turn was the start of a conservative reaction against the New Deal and the welfare state and the associated growth in state intervention, expenditure and regulation as well as social liberalisation: a 'conservative counter-revolution' with deep and powerful long-term effects. Neoliberal theory was essentially a device to explain and justify this reaction (as the quotes above from George Monbiot and Mike Conczal suggest). The recent rise in 'authoritarian populism' can be seen as a societal response to the policies associated with this reaction, a response exploited by populist demagogues like Donald Trump and Boris Johnson.[4]

The rest of this chapter explains how this book is organised.

Chapter 2, 'Markets in Higher Education', considers the meaning, extent and impact of the application of the theory of markets to the provision of British higher education since 1980, symbolised by the introduction of 'full cost' fees from 2012. It uses this case study to introduce the main tenets of Neoliberalism: essentially, that everything and everyone is a piece of capital to be developed and expanded just like any other piece of capital.

Chapter 3, 'The Impact of Neoliberalism', assesses the impact of the main policies associated with Neoliberalism (deregulation, privatisation, tax reduction, welfare constraint and deflation) on inequality and economic growth as key features of a healthy society. It considers the evidence that these policies have increased inequality and reduced growth, as well as causing many other detriments to society, the economy and the political system.

Chapters 4 and 5, 'Explaining the Neoliberal Turn', discuss some of the theories that seek to account for the Neoliberal Turn. Chapter 4 looks at 'structural' theories that emphasise underlying, longer-term developments such as globalisation and technological change. Chapter 5 looks at 'institutional' explanations that focus on political actors, institutions and cultures.

Chapter 6, 'Authoritarian Populism and Its Sources', considers the post-1980s resurgence of authoritarian populism: authoritarian values cloaked in populist rhetoric. It argues that, in its current manifestation, authoritarian populism is essentially a societal response to Neoliberalism and the policies associated with it (including, since the 2008–09 crisis, austerity). It notes that it is already doing great damage to our democratic political systems. It distinguishes 'cultural' and 'economic' explanations. It concludes that the recent rise reflects both cultural and economic drivers, but that it will only be halted through a serious reset of our political arrangements.

Chapter 7, 'The Conservative Counter-revolution', begins by enumerating the key features of conservative thought drawing especially on the work of Professor Corey Robin (2018). It explains and expands on the idea of the conservative counter-revolution, of which Neoliberal theory has been a useful tool. It notes that the term 'conservative' is a misnomer, that conservative parties can be radical or even revolutionary where there is a serious risk of power being broadened away from elites or dominant groups, and that the long-run Conservative/Republican reaction to the welfare state/New Deal is just such a case. It shows how Neoliberalism has been used by those elites/groups to challenge and partially undo the welfare Keynesianism of the early postwar period. It explains how this has been done and how, in Britain and America, the mass of the population has been moved to support policies that are seemingly against its economic or class interest. This book concludes with some suggestions as to how, with appropriate learning and leadership, progressive political parties might begin to reverse this process—a progressive counter-counter-revolution.

NOTES

1. *Levelling Up the United Kingdom* Department for Levelling Up, Housing and Communities 2 February 2022 (see Chap. 7).
2. See Harvey (2005), Lansley (2011), Gordon (2016), Pettifor (2017) and Dorling (2021) for general surveys. For the effect on world trade, see Pettifor (2006). For savings, see Eggertsson et al. (2018). For the association of financialisation with financial crises, see Reid et al. (2017). For market concentration, see Tepper with Hearn (2019). For fraud, see Callahan (2004); Whyte and Wiegratz (2016); Toms (2019). For crime generally, see Wilkinson and Pickett (2009 and 2018) and Dorward (2019). For inequality, see Piketty (2014 and 2020), Atkinson (2015), Baker (2016), Brown, R. (2017). For trust, see Edelman Trust (2022).
3. Prasad (2018: 30) quotes President Kennedy in 1962:

It is a paradoxical truth that tax rates are too high today and tax revenues are too low and the soundest way to raise the revenues in the long run is to cut the rates now. The experience of a number of European countries and Japan [has] borne this out. This country's own experience with tax reduction in 1954 has borne this out. And the reason is that only full employment can balance the budget, and tax reduction can pave the way to that employment. The purpose of cutting taxes now is not to incur a budget deficit, but to achieve the more prosperous, expanding economy which can bring a budget surplus.

4. We shall consider in Chap. 7 the irony that most of these individuals have elite backgrounds and once in power have often canvassed pro-elite policies.

REFERENCES

Apple, R. W. (1984, November 14). Macmillan, at 90, rouses the Lords. *The New York Times.*

Atkinson, A. B. (2015). *Inequality: What can be done?* Harvard University Press.

Baker, D. (2016). *Rigged: How globalization and the rules of the modern economy were structured to make the rich richer.* Center for Economic and Policy Research.

BBC News Channel. (2005, March 26). *Jim Callaghan: A life in quotes.* Retrieved September 28, 2017, from http://news.bbc.co.uk/1/ukpolitics/3288907.stm

Brown, R. (2017). *The inequality crisis: What are the facts and what we can do about it.* Policy Press.

Callahan, D. (2004). *The cheating culture: Why more Americans are doing wrong to get ahead.* Houghton Mifflin.

Dorling, D. (2021). *Slowdown: The end of the great acceleration – and why it's a good thing.* Yale University Press.

Dorward, J. (2019, April 28). Industrial collapse of the 1980s led crime to rise, study finds. *The Observer.*

Edelman Trust. (2022, January 25). *Edelman Trust Barometer 2021.* Retrieved February 28, 2022, from https://www.edelman.com/sites/g/files/aatuss191/files/2022-01/2022%20Edelman%20Trust%20Barometer%.FINAL_Jan25.pdf.

Eggertsson, G., Robbins, J. A., & Getz Wold, E. (2018). *Kaldor and Piketty's facts: The rise of monopoly power in the United States.* Center for Equitable Growth.

Gordon, R. J. (2016). *The rise and fall of American growth: The US standard of living since the civil war.* Princeton University Press.

Harvey, D. (2005). *A brief history of Neoliberalism.* Oxford University Press.

Konczal, M. (2021). *Freedom from the market: America's fight to liberate itself from the grip of the invisible hand.* The New Press.

Lansley, S. (2011). *The cost of inequality: Three decades of the super-rich and the economy.* Gibson Square.

Monbiot, G. (2016). *How did we get into this mess?* Verso.

Pettifor, A. (2006). *The coming first world debt crisis*. Palgrave Macmillan.

Pettifor, A. (2017). *The production of money: How to break the power of the bankers*. Verso.

Piketty, T. (2014). *Capital in the twenty-first century*. Harvard University Press.

Piketty, T. (2020). *Capital and ideology*. The Belknap Press of Harvard University Press.

Prasad, M. (2018). *Starving the beast: Ronald Reagan and the tax cut revolution*. Russell Sage.

Reid, J., Burns, N., & Chanda, S. (2017). *Long-term asset return study: An ever changing world*. Deutsche Bank AG. http://www.tramuntalegria.com/wp-content/uploads/2017/09/Long-Term-Asset-Return-Study-The-Next-Financial-Crisis-db.pdf.

Robin, C. (2018). *The reactionary mind: Conservatism from Edmund Burke to Donald Trump* (2nd ed.). Oxford University Press.

Tepper, J., & Hearn, D. (2019). *The myth of capitalism: Monopolies and the death of competition*. Wiley.

Toms, S. (2019). Financial scandals: A historical overview. *Accounting and Business Research, 49*(5), 477–499. https://doi.org/10.1080/0001478 8.2019.1610591

Whyte, D., & Wiegratz, J. (2016). *Neoliberalism and the moral economy of fraud*. Routledge.

Wilkinson, R., & Pickett, K. (2009). *The spirit level: Why equal societies almost always do better*. Allen Lane.

Wilkinson, R., & Pickett, K. (2018). *The inner level*. Allen Lane.

CHAPTER 2

Markets in Higher Education

Abstract This chapter describes how the theory of markets has been applied to the provision of British (and particularly English) higher education since 1980. It concludes with an outline of Neoliberal beliefs as further background for the rest of the book.

Keywords Higher education • Markets • Neoliberalism • Quasi-Markets • Universities

> *Where effective competition can be created, it is a better means of guiding individual efforts than any other* (Hayek, *1944*: 27, quoted in Marginson, *2004*: 207).
>
> *Unleashing the forces of consumerism is the best single way we've got of restoring high academic standards* (David Willetts, Minister for Higher Education, quoted in Morgan, *2012*).
>
> *More than mere economic policy, neoliberalism is a governing social and political rationality that submits all human activities, values, institutions, and practices to market principles. It formulates everything in terms of capital investment and appreciation (including and especially humans themselves), whether a teenager building a resume for college, a twenty-something seeking a mate, a working mother returning to school, or a corporation buying carbon offsets. As a governing rationality, neoliberalism extends from the management of*

the state itself to the soul of the subject; it renders health, education,
transportation, nature, and art into individual consumer goods, and
converts patients, students, drivers, athletes, and museum-goers alike
into entrepreneurs of their own needs and desires who consume or invest
in those goods (Brown, W. *2011a*: 118).
The central defining characteristic of all neoliberal technique is its
hostility to the ambiguity of political discourse, and a commitment to
the explicitness and transparency of quantitative, economic indicators,
*of which the market price system is the model. Neoliberalism is **the***
pursuit of the disenchantment of politics by economics (Davies, *2014*:
4, original author's emphasis).

2.1   The Theory of Markets

In economic theory, a market is a means of social coordination where supply and demand for a good or service are balanced through the price
mechanism. Consumers choose between the alternatives on offer on the
basis of suitability: not only price but also quality and availability. Suppliers
adjust their product to accommodate these preferences or leave the market. Markets are held to provide both greater 'static efficiency' (the ratio
of outputs to inputs at any one time) and greater 'dynamic efficiency'
(sustaining a higher rate of growth over time through product and process
innovation and better management) than any alternative (for a recent
overview, see Coyle, 2020).

2.2   Markets in Higher Education: In Theory

Although market theory was first developed in relation to the demand and
supply of private goods and services, it was not long before its proponents
sought to extend it to the public sector, and indeed, Milton Friedman's
published proposals for state schools to be funded through full-cost education vouchers date from the early 1960s (Friedman, 1962).[1]

In a market system of higher education, what is provided is determined
neither by the state nor by the academy. Entry to the market is lightly
regulated. Students have a considerable amount of information about the
courses on offer and there is plenty of competition for their custom. There
are no limits on what institutions are able to charge for their courses or on
how many students they are able to enrol. The costs of teaching are met
entirely or mostly through tuition fees that are set to match institutions'

costs. Students meet these fees (and their living costs while studying) from their own or their families' resources (Brown, R. 2011b).

The UK, and particularly England, has moved closer to this market model than almost any other major system (for a recent survey, see Branch & Christiansen, 2021). The author's 2013 book with Dr. Helen Carasso traced this process back to the decision of the Thatcher Government in 1979 to remove the subsidy that had previously been applied to overseas students' fees. Subsequent key steps were the following:[2]

1. The separation of the funding of teaching from the funding of research, enabling selective funding of both activities, from 1986.
2. The increase in the level of the (still-subsidised) tuition fee for home students, and the matching reduction in the level of the Government grant towards institutions' teaching costs, from 1989.
3. The introduction of 'top-up' loans to supplement student maintenance grants, from 1990.
4. The abolition of the 'binary line' in 1992, enabling the former polytechnics and some other institutions to acquire a university title.
5. The introduction of 'top-up' fees of £1000 from 1998.
6. The modification of the rules for university title in 2004 to enable colleges without powers to award research degrees (including the author's own institution) to become universities (previously, applicant institutions had to have the powers to award both taught degrees and research degrees—MPhil, PhD).
7. The introduction of 'variable' fees of up to £3000 in 2006.
8. The raising of the full-time tuition fee to £9000 from 2012 (it is now £9250) and the removal of most subsidies for institutions' teaching costs. Direct Government funding remains for particular policy areas and Government priorities such as equal opportunities, but this is a voucher system in all but name. Subsidised Government loans are available to help with students' tuition and living costs although the level of non-repayment means that the revenue from interest charges and repayments will never cover the total cost of provision.[3]
9. Parallel changes to the rules for degree awarding powers and university title to enable more providers to enter the market. As a result, the UK now has 175 institutions with powers to award their own degrees.[4]

10. The final abolition in 2015–16 of Government limits on the student numbers recruited by each institution.
11. The establishment in 2018 of the Office for Students to operate a regulatory regime very similar to that for the privatised utilities.[5]

2.3   The Higher Education Market in Practice

The 2013 book offered an assessment of the impact of these changes at that time (this was before the 2012 reforms had begun to kick in). The authors found that UK universities and colleges had undoubtedly become more efficient, more enterprising and more responsive to external stakeholders. There had been a small reduction in 'horizontal' institutional diversity/differentiation (there were now too many institutions offering like-for-like courses/awards) but an increase in 'vertical' institutional diversity (greater differentiation by status). Increasing selectivity and concentration in research funding had made a major contribution to both developments, the most 'research-intensive' institutions using their performance in research to enhance their resources and general status.[6]

However, whilst there was no definitive evidence, increased competition for students coupled with a long-term reduction in funding per student as the system expanded had almost certainly led to a reduction in the quality of education received by students. Moreover, there were some indications that increased research selectivity had damaged not only teaching but also other forms of scholarly inquiry (such as the production of textbooks) that were not covered by the periodic assessments. Finally, there was an inverse relationship between institutional selectivity, resourcing and status, on the one hand, and the recruitment of students from the lowest-income households, on the other (Adams, 2021; Institute for Fiscal Studies, 2021).[7]

These conclusions remain robust. Two of the detriments are of particular significance in the context of this book.

First, marketisation reinforces, and even exacerbates, existing resourcing and status differentials between higher education institutions, subjects and modes of study. This is hardly a surprise. Markets are intended to produce winners and losers. But markets are particularly problematic in higher education because of the difficulty of specifying the product or creating proper quality indicators. As a wise American expert once wrote:

Higher education is a process masquerading as an outcome. (Trow, 1992)

This means that just like consumers in other markets without direct product information, students resort to proxies, and the one they fall back on is institutional status (which is usually associated with resources). This then reinforces the differentials (Brown, R. 2012). At the same time, institutions divert income to status-raising activities (such as shiny new refectories or sports halls), resources that could and should have been used to improve the quality of their teaching and research (Brown, R. 2014).[8]

The second detriment, which has had rather more attention from scholars and commentators (e.g., Newfield, 2011), is the supersession of the 'liberal' view of higher education as a means of intellectual development and maturation—including through the direct exposure of students to knowledge obtained through research and scholarship—by one which sees higher education as being about the development of human capital in the interests of economic growth and efficiency: higher education as just another vehicle for capital accumulation.[9]

The liberal view will be forever associated with the famous Robbins Report (Committee on Higher Education, 1963) although Lord Robbins himself was, ironically, a leading Neoliberal.[10] The economic view has been reflected in nearly every statement of Government policy since the 1985 Green Paper *The Development of Higher Education into the 1990s* (Department of Education and Science, 1985). It has led to the publication of economic outcomes by subject and provider,[11] as well as official attempts to steer institutions and students towards subjects that the Government regards as economically relevant—usually, science and technology—at the expense of those that it doesn't—arts, humanities, media and non-quantitative social science.

2.4   Neoliberalism: Core Beliefs

As will very shortly become clear, these changes in the provision of UK higher education have reflected pretty closely the key precepts of Neoliberalism. However, there does not appear to be any generally accepted definition.[12]

For the purpose of this discussion, 'Neoliberalism' is held to embrace the following beliefs:

1. **Markets** are far better at generating and allocating resources than governments or states. In a modern economy, only markets can generate the necessary information. Where they cannot be transferred

to the private sector, state-owned suppliers like schools, colleges and hospitals should be made subject to market or 'quasi-market' (Le Grand & Bartlett, 1993) competition.

2. **Deregulation:** Domestic and international barriers to the free movement of goods, services, capital, people, information and ideas should be the minimum possible. Business should be able to get on with the job of creating wealth with a minimum amount of regulatory interference ('red tape') in its affairs.

3. **Privatisation:** Wherever possible, the entities supplying goods and services should be privately owned. This is necessary both to reduce public expenditure and to increase efficiency.

4. **Tax reduction:** Wherever possible, the costs of services should be met by those who consume them (such as students). Taxes should be levied in proportion to the extent of use, not to the ability to pay. Generally, the burden of taxation should be reduced, ideally to the level needed just to pay for certain core state functions: defence, internal security and the administration of justice. This will increase economic growth and prosperity as successful entrepreneurs use the resources that are released to invest and innovate (previously, such investment was 'crowded out' by public spending). The reductions in tax rates will also increase tax revenues: by increasing wealth, the additional incentives to innovate and take risks will more than pay for themselves (the 'Laffer curve').[13] The additional wealth created will 'trickle down' to the rest of society with beneficial effects for all.

5. **Welfare** programmes should provide a very basic level of protection from ill-health, unemployment, etc. The main purpose of the welfare state should be to incentivise work as the best form of social security. Great efforts should be made to prevent or root out benefits fraud.

6. **The management of the economy** should aim to reduce inflation, if necessary at the cost of higher unemployment. The main barrier to economic growth is not lack of demand or purchasing power, but supply-side inefficiency and lack of responsiveness. Government intervention in the economy should therefore be confined to measures to improve the supply side. The austerity policies followed in both countries since 2008–09 represent a continuation of this thinking.

2.5 CONCLUSION

In this chapter we reviewed the market-based reforms of UK higher education since 1979 as a way of introducing the core beliefs of Neoliberalism. In Chap. 3 we shall consider the wider impact of the Neoliberal social and economic policies introduced in Britain and America since the late 1970s.

NOTES

1. In a recent (2021) paper, Nancy MacLean shows how Friedman's efforts to privatise education (to which state-funded vouchers were an end) buttressed efforts in the South to resist the desegregation of schools that followed the Supreme Court's judgement in Brown v. Board of Education (1954).
2. It should be noted that 6–9 have not been applied, or have been only partially applied, in Scotland (Bruce, 2016).
3. The Government has recently announced plans to change the loan terms to reduce the shortfall (Department for Education, 2022). The changes will take the loans system closer to a 'graduate tax' (Barr, 2009). In spite of the Government's professed belief in expanding access from low-income households, the new arrangements are seriously regressive. Low- to middle-income graduates could be made about £20,000 worse off over their lifetime whilst the highest earners could be £25,000 better off (Johnson, P. 2022).
4. Retrieved 2 January 2022 from https://www.gov.uk/check-university-award-degree-recognised-bodies.
5. There has over time been a shift in the balance of regulation in higher education away from self-regulation to regulation by the state and the market (Brown, R. 2004, 2018). This has culminated for the moment in proposals by the Office for Students (January 2022) for all institutions to be judged by 'minimum acceptable outcomes'. As we shall see later (Chap. 7), this inconsistency between Neoliberal theory about the role of the state and Neoliberal governing practice is by no means confined to higher education.
6. As described in Brown with Carasso (2013: 41–70), since 1987 direct government funding of university research has reflected periodic quality assessments: initially the Research Assessment Exercise, now the Research Excellence Framework. Over time this funding has become increasingly concentrated so that a small handful of (generally, long-established) institutions (mostly in London and the South East) receives a high proportion of the total.

7. Although successive governments have directed their fire at the leading universities' admissions procedures, the fundamental cause is socioeconomic inequality and its reflection in school and college provision: the opportunities and support for students and their families. This goes far wider than the fact that the private schools continue to send disproportionate numbers of students to Oxford and Cambridge and other 'top' universities. Brian Barry's summary remains as accurate now as when it was first published:

> *Whereas a socially just education system would minimise the effects on children's opportunities of their parents' social and economic position, the current set-up in Britain operates at every point to expand the advantages of parents with education, money and high aspirations. "School choice" is just the final straw, in which the effects of parental advantages and disadvantages are multiplied by placing an enormous premium on know-how and resources* (Barry, 2005: 66; see also, Dorling, 2018).

8. Institutions also put enormous effort into manipulating and massaging the statistics that underlie the various performance 'league tables'. As Davies (2020: 18) says: 'Under neoliberal conditions, all action becomes dictated by a single question … what will this mean for my ratings?' For the enhanced pursuit of status under Neoliberalism, see Storr (2021).

9. For the 'economic ideology of higher education', see Salter and Tapper (1994).

10. In his account of the historical origins of Neoliberalism, Slobodian (2018: 102) quotes Robbins as saying 'shared precarity should be the foundation of world unity'. Precarity is a continuing Neoliberal trope. George Monbiot (2020) quotes Peter Hargreaves, a billionaire who donated £3.2 m to the Brexit Leave campaign, as explaining that, after Brexit, 'We will get out there and we will become incredibly successful because we will be insecure again. And insecurity is fantastic'. Recent research at the Nuffield Political Centre (Green and de Geus, 2022) suggests that economic insecurity is as much of a dividing line between voters as age and level of education.

11. Retrieved 2 January 2022 from https://explore-education-statistics.service.gov.uk/find-statistics/graduate-outcomes-leo-provider-level-data.

12. For a comprehensive discussion of terms and terminology, see Treanor (2009); for the nearest thing to a Neoliberal 'manifesto', see Peters, C. (1982). Harvey (2005) is as good an introduction as any.

13. The Laffer Curve is a theory devised by the US economist Arthur Laffer that purports to demonstrate that, counter-intuitively, tax revenues increase as tax rates reduce. However, there is plenty of evidence that it is flawed (e.g., Piketty et al., 2011).

REFERENCES

Adams, J. (2021, November 24). England's most prestigious universities failing to boost social mobility, IFS finds. *The Guardian on-line*. Retrieved November 24, 2021, from https://www.theguardian.com/education/2021/nov/24/englands-most-prestigious-universities-failing-to-boost-social-mobiliyt-ifs-finds

Barr, N. (2009, March 24). A graduate tax is for life, not just for a few years. *The Guardian*.

Barry, B. (2005). *Why social justice matters*. Polity.

Branch, J. D., & Christiansen, B. (2021). *The marketisation of higher education: Concepts, cases and criticisms*. Palgrave Macmillan.

Brown, R. (2004). *Quality assurance in higher education: The UK experience since 2004*. Routledge Falmer.

Brown, W. (2011a). Neoliberalized knowledge. *History of the Present, 1*(1), 113–129.

Brown, R. (Ed.). (2011b). *Higher education and the market*. Routledge.

Brown, R. (2012). *The myth of student choice*. University of West London Institute for Teaching, Innovation and Learning Annual Lecture 5th December.

Brown, R. (2014). The real crisis in higher education. *Higher Education Review, 46*(3), 4–25.

Brown, R. (2018). Changing patterns of accountability in the UK – From QA to TEF. In E. Hazelkorn, A. C. McCormick, & H. Coates (Eds.), *Research handbook on quality, performance and accountability in higher education* (pp. 457–471). Edward Elgar.

Brown, R., & Carasso, H. (2013). *Everything for sale? The marketisation of UK higher education*. Routledge.

Bruce, A. (2016). Scotland and the higher education market. In P. John & J. Fanghangel (Eds.), *Dimensions of marketisation in higher education* (pp. 57–66). Routledge.

Committee on Higher Education. (1963). *Higher Education*. HMSO.

Coyle, D. (2020). *Markets, state and people: Economics for public policy*. Princeton University Press.

Davies, W. (2014). *The limits of Neoliberalism: Authority, sovereignty and the logic of competition*. Sage.

Davies, W. (2020). *This is not normal: The collapse of liberal Britain*. Verso.

Department for Education. (2022, February 24). *Fairer higher education system for students and taxpayers*. Retrieved February 28, 2022, from https://www.gov.uk/government/news/fairer-higher-education-system-for-students-and-taxpayers.

Department of Education and Science. (1985). *Higher Education into the 1990s* Cmnd 9524. HMSO

Dorling, D. (2018). *Peak inequality: Britain's ticking time bomb*. Policy Press.
Friedman, M. (1962). *Capitalism and freedom*. Chicago University Press.
Green, R., & de Geus, R. (2022). *Red wall, red herring?* Nuffield Political Research Centre.
Harvey, D. (2005). *A brief history of Neoliberalism*. Oxford University Press.
Hayek, F. (1944). *The road to Serfdom*. Routledge and Kegan Paul.
Institute for Fiscal Studies. (2021). *Which university degrees are best for intergenerational mobility?* Institute for Fiscal Studies. https://ifs.org.uk/uploads/Which-university-degrees-are-best-for-intergenerational-mobility.pdf.
Johnson, P. (2022, February 28). Changes to university fees are set to penalise lower-earning graduates. *The Times*.
Le Grand, J., & Bartlett, W. (1993). *Quasi-markets and social policy*. Macmillan.
Marginson, S. (2004). Australian higher education: National and global markets. In P. N. Teixeira, B. Jongbloed, D. Dill, & A. Amaral (Eds.), *Markets in higher education: Rhetoric or reality?* (pp. 207–240). Kluwer Academic Publishers.
Monbiot, G. (2020, November 25). There is a civil war in capitalism and we're the collateral damage. *The Guardian Journal*.
Morgan, J. (2012, October 11). Wake up to the new world, declares Willetts. *Times Higher Education*.
Newfield, C. (2011). *Unmaking the public university: The forty-year assault on the middle class*. Harvard University Press.
Peters, C. (1982, September 5). A Neo-Liberal's Manifesto. *The Washington Post*.
Piketty, T., Saez, E., & Stantcheva, S. (2011, December 8). Taxing the 1%: Why the top tax rate could be over 80%. VoxEU.org. https://voxeu.org/article/taxing-1-why-top-tax-rate-could-be-over-80.
Salter, B., & Tapper, T. (1994). *The state and higher education*. Woburn Press.
Slobodian, Q. (2018). *Globalists: The end of empire and the birth of Neoliberalism*. Harvard University Press.
Storr, W. (2021). *The status game: On social status and how we use it*. William Collins.
Treanor, P. (2009). *Neoliberalism: Origins, theory, definition*. Retrieved November 22, 2017, from http://web.inter.nl/users/Paul.Treanor/neoliberalism.html.
Trow, M. (1992). Aspects of quality in higher education. Paper prepared for a conference *Quality and the Renewal of Higher Education*, Stockholm, 12–13 March.

CHAPTER 3

The Impact of Neoliberalism

Abstract In Chap. 2 we introduced the theory of the market and described its application to the provision of UK (and especially English) higher education, in particular by transferring the costs on to individual students/graduates as users/beneficiaries. We observed that the higher education policies of successive British Governments since the late 1970s reflected pretty well the core precepts of Neoliberalism that we outlined. In this chapter we look at the wider impact of Neoliberalism in Britain and America over this period, focusing on socioeconomic inequality and economic growth. This is on the basis that (a) a healthy developed country should experience steady economic growth and (b) the benefits should be widely and fairly spread across the population, so ensuring that there is some relationship between what people contribute to society and what they get out of it.

However, it is a fact that over this period Britain and America have experienced higher levels of inequality, and lower levels of economic growth, than in the preceding 40 or so years. Both socioeconomic inequality and economic growth are complex phenomena with many causes. But

---

I am very grateful to Stewart Lansley for drawing my attention to this quote.

there can be little doubt that Neoliberal policies of deregulation, privatisation, tax reductions and welfare cutbacks, on top of generally deflationary macroeconomic policies, have meant that inequality has been higher, and growth lower, than would otherwise have been the case. Levels of poverty are also higher. (For the relationship between inequality and poverty, see Hills et al., *Understanding the relationship between poverty and inequality*. Centre for Analysis of Social Exclusion, London School of Economics (2019). Lansley, *The richer, the poorer: How Britain enriched the few and failed the poor*. Policy Press. (2022) observes: *With many of the mechanisms that deliver wealth at the top also the source of squeezed incomes at the bottom, periods of high inequality have been strongly associated with high rates of impoverishment.*)

Keywords Economic growth • Income inequality • Inequality • Neoliberalism • Poverty • Wealth inequality

> *A society with less inequality will be socially more cohesive, have greater social mobility, be better educated, more tolerant, healthier, have less crime, be more environmentally sustainable, be wealthier and more productive, and will have a better political system, where ordinary citizens are involved in governance in some way, and where the policies adopted reflect in significant degree the views and interests of all its members rather than of a small, wealthy subset* (Brown, R. 2017: 47). *Making the rich poorer does not make the poor rich, but it does make the state stronger ... The pursuit of income equality will turn this country into a totalitarian slum* (Joseph, 1976: 23).

3.1   INEQUALITY

In *The Inequality Crisis: What Are the Facts and What We Can Do About It* (Brown, R. 2017), the author noted that while inequality of income had risen in most Western (and many other) countries since the late 1970s, Britain and America were the major high-income countries with the greatest such inequality, albeit with different trajectories (in Britain there had been a sharp rise in the mid- and late-1980s and then a plateauing, whereas in the US the rise was more gradual). According to the latest OECD (Organisation for Economic Cooperation and Development) data (2020), this remains the case.[1]

There had been a particularly striking increase in the share of total income taken by the top 1% of households (for the importance of the top 1%, see Atkinson et al., 2011). In the UK, according to the most recent Office for National Statistics (ONS) data (2021a), the top 1% of households accounted in 2019–20 for 8.3% of all income. The current (2018) US equivalent is 22 (Saez, 2020).[2]

In both countries, inequality of wealth is even greater than inequality of income. In the UK, in 2018–20 each of the richest 1% owned an average of £3.6 m, 230 times higher than the £15,400 or less for the least wealthy 10% (ONS, 2022). In the US in 2021, the top centile owned 26.8% of all household wealth (Federal Reserve, 2021). It should be noted that because of the extent to which the very wealthy disguise their wealth, these figures almost certainly understate the degree of inequality (Zucman, 2016).[3] Moreover, it appears that Covid has reinforced these inequalities (Caddick & Stirling, 2021).

There was a similar story with the functional distribution of national income between labour and capital: functional inequality. In both countries, there had been a significant fall in the share taken by wages and a rise in that taken by capital: interest, rents and dividends. In the UK, the percentage share of GDP taken by wages and employee remuneration fell from an average of 69.9% between 1955 and 1969 to an average of 59.9% between 1970 and 2019 (ONS, 2021b); the US percentages were 65 and 59 (St Louis Fed, 2021). This was particularly striking because in Britain (and in most other advanced countries) higher incomes—included in the wage share—have of course risen over the period (in Britain, disproportionately in finance).

These shifts reflected the fact that wages had failed to keep pace with inflation or rises in productivity. There had in effect been a massive upward transfer of wealth from the great majority who are wage earners to a small minority whose income comes mainly—or partly, because many of the 'working rich' also earn high incomes—from their capital. Overall, there had been a compression in the wages on which most of the population rely, and a strengthening of the position of the well-off (and especially the top 1% and 0.1%) through increased returns to capital, much higher levels of top remuneration (e.g., for CEOs) and much lower rates of tax.[4]

This rise in inequality had had a range of costs and detriments. The social and educational impacts—the association of increased inequality with a large number of social and educational problems, such as declining social mobility and life expectancy—had received a good deal of attention from scholars like Wilkinson and Pickett (2009, 2018), Deaton (2015), Marmot (2015) and Dorling (2018). However, the economic and political effects were less studied.

Traditionally, the main justification for inequality was economic. To quote the then Mayor of London:

> *Some measure of inequality is essential for the spirit of envy and keeping up with the Joneses that is, like greed, a valuable spur to economic activity.* (Johnson, B. 2013)

To judge by the Prime Minister's more recent remarks about Britain's Covid vaccine programme being driven by greed (BBC, 2021), this remains his view.

As good a statement as any of how inequality actually damages growth can be found in Dabla-Norris et al. (2015: 8–9). Inequality reduces the ability of lower-income households to stay healthy and accumulate physical and human capital, for example by investing in education and training. It dampens investment by fuelling economic, financial and political instability. It can lead to a backlash against market-based policies for growth (see Chap. 6). And it hampers the reduction of poverty (see also Wolf, 2014). It has also been argued that inequality causes 'underconsumption' and trade wars as countries with high levels of inequality seek to recycle the excess savings (of the wealthy) that are the inevitable corollary of great inequality (Klein & Pettis, 2020).

Azmanova (2019) argues that, together, globalisation, technological change and reduced social safety nets have extended to previously successful labour market insiders the conditions of uncertainty and instability that were previously experienced only by the less fortunate. This development has gone well beyond inequality although inequality of wealth in particular is a major part of it because only wealth offers proper protection against risk. Most seriously of all, the association of economic power with political power threatens to replace democracy with oligarchy and/or authoritarian populism (as we shall see in Chap. 6). Finally, there is growing concern about the contribution of greater economic inequality to climate change, with a tiny segment of the population being responsible for a high proportion of carbon emissions (Chancel, 2017; Oswald et al., 2020; United Nations Environment Programme, 2020).

What had caused this rise in inequality? The author identified both 'structural' and 'institutional' factors.

The structural factors included:

- globalisation, the progressive removal of barriers to the cross-border movement of goods, services and people;
- 'skill-biased technological change' putting a premium on higher level skills and qualifications;
- changes in the organisation of work, the 'gig economy';
- changes in household structure (for instance, the increase in the number of single-headed households and the greater likelihood of people choosing partners in the same earnings bracket: 'assortative mating');
- the growth in 'winner-take-all' markets (Frank & Cook, 2010) where small differences in performance translate into large differences in reward, higher education being a good example and
- capitalism itself, with its relentless drive to extend production and cut costs through technological innovation.

The institutional factors were:

- the Neoliberal policies pursued in most Western economies since the mid- and late-70s and (at least until quite recently) endorsed by the major international intergovernmental organisations (the 'Washington Consensus');[5]
- the changing role of labour market organisations (the weakening of the trade unions);
- financialisation[6] and rent-seeking (see below, this chapter) and
- macroeconomic policy, where the focus since the late-1970s had been on reducing inflation rather than unemployment.

On the basis of the international evidence and comparisons, the author concluded that whilst the main structural factors had affected most Western countries, the fact that the increase in inequality had not occurred equally in all of them—and had not been historically continuous even in the more unequal—suggested that institutional factors might also be relevant. The key to understanding why inequality was now so much greater in the major Anglophone economies than it had been since the War appeared to lie in the Neoliberal reforms associated with Margaret Thatcher and Ronald Reagan in Britain and America. The deflationary macroeconomic policies associated with these reforms—austerity, anyone?—had reinforced these impacts, as had an associated concentration of political (and media) power, especially in the US (another important issue to which we shall return in Chap. 7).[7]

In spite of some measures to ameliorate some of the most extreme features of marketisation, neither the Blair/Brown Governments in the UK nor the Clinton or Obama administrations in the US had really challenged the Neoliberal hegemony (cf. Kuttner, 2018: 149–179). The major country where Neoliberal policies were first applied on a large scale was post-Pinochet Chile from 1973. The disastrous effects for the economy and society, from which Chile is still recovering, are described in Nancy MacLean's, 2017 book *Democracy in Chains:* 154–168 (see also Lazo-Gonzalez, 2019).

Finally, the author noted the theory of the American political sociologist, Monica Prasad (2006), that one reason why Neoliberal thinking and policies had become so influential in Britain and America lay in their political economies. Britain and America had 'adversarial' political structures that defined labour and capital as natural enemies, positioned the middle and working classes in opposition to one another (the middle classes paying for benefits for the work-shy), and had structures that provided the potential to ally the majority of voters with market-friendly policies, as well as incentives for politicians to exploit the differences. Per contra, for different reasons but ultimately bound up with the need for postwar rebuilding, France and Germany had more corporatist and consensual political and governance structures. This was 'path dependence' with a vengeance.[8]

The author sees no reason to change these conclusions, except perhaps to give greater weight to market concentration and rent-seeking as important contributory factors to inequality.[9]

3.1.1   Market Concentration

The Inequality Crisis referred to work in 2015 by the then Chair of the US President's Council of Economic Advisers that linked increased concentration in many market sectors to greater inequality (Furman & Orszag, 2015). This analysis was confirmed in a 2019 book by Jonathan Tepper with Denise Hearn. This shows how there has over the past 30 or so years been a significant increase in market concentration—through monopolistic or oligopolistic behaviour—in many sectors of the US economy. This was due principally to the cycle of deregulation that began under President

Reagan and which was also at least partially responsible for the 2008 financial crisis (Tooze, 2018).

Socially, increased market concentration means there is a growing discrepancy between the wages of workers in increasingly monopsonistic (single employer) labour markets (reinforced by globalisation, especially after China joined the World Trade Organisation in 2001), and the returns to the owners of capital. The producer surplus that reflects this increased market power accrues chiefly to shareholders and senior executives. These firms then use their economic muscle politically to consolidate their market dominance, Silicon Valley being a case in point (Foroohar, 2020). All of this is of course completely contrary to the Neoliberal shibboleth of 'free and fair competition' (for a similar analysis, see Lindsey & Teles, 2019, Shambaugh et al., 2018, and Phillipon, 2019).

Market concentration also has a strong geopolitical dimension. In particular, it weakens relationships between local communities and business, with mergers and takeovers hollowing out many local economies. Tepper with Hearn (2019: 73) reproduces a map showing a very close association between counties that voted for Donald Trump in 2016 and commuting zones with a high labour concentration (travel-to-work areas with few local employers).

Barry C. Lynn (2021) argues that increased market concentration in the US is part of a wider international trend, the consequences of which are apparent in the post-Covid shortage of computer chips. He suggests that instead of resorting to protectionism to bring production home, the US should work to break concentrations of power wherever they occur in the international economic system.[10]

3.1.2   Rent-Seeking

Tepper with Hearn also mentions the enormous subsidies and tax breaks enjoyed by major US corporations. In the author's book on inequality, reference was made to an estimate by Dr. Kevin Farnsworth (2015) that in 2012–13, 'corporate welfare'—'official' subsidies, capital grants, tax benefits, hidden transport subsidies, insurance and advocacy, additional energy subsidies and procurement subsidies—was worth about £93bn annually in the UK. There was also legal corporate tax avoidance of £12bn (it has not been possible to obtain an update).

Simon Nixon pointed out in *The Times* recently (2022) that the post-Brexit Subsidy Control Bill currently going through Parliament is significantly less transparent and allows regulators greater discretion, than the previous EU arrangements for monitoring and controlling state aids.[11]

Even so, companies continue to lobby for tax breaks. But whilst business tax rates have been falling in both Britain and America for many years, there has also been less investment. So it looks as if the former US Treasury Secretary, Lawrence Summers, was basically correct when he wrote in November 2017 that 'corporate tax reduction serves only to reward monopoly profits, other rents or past investments' (Summers, 2017; see also Fleming, 2017).

3.2   The Management of the Economy

As noted in Chap. 1, whilst inflation has been lower, on nearly every other recognised economic measure—growth, unemployment, investment and productivity—the performance of the British and American (and many other Western) economies since 1980 has been much worse than previously.[12]

There has also been much greater instability, with a series of bubbles and busts, above all the 2008–09 crisis. We have had a long period of 'secular stagnation' (Summers, 2013), a period of persistent insufficiency of demand which has been highly resistant to conventional monetary policy (e.g., through lower interest rates) and even unconventional monetary policy (quantitative easing).[13]

Over this period two alternative ways of restoring growth have been canvassed: the 'supply-side' use of market competition and consumer information to make producers more efficient, and the 'demand-side' deployment of government funding and actions to repair weaknesses in the underlying demand-generating process: 'structural Keynesianism' (Palley, 2012).

The latter fits the facts better. Prior to the Neoliberal reforms, the main engine of demand growth was wage growth. Demand growth was income-led. This had led to full employment, which in turn led to more investment, productivity and further wage growth. But deregulation and disinflation together broke the link between wage growth and productivity growth, with demand being sustained only through borrowing and asset price inflation: credit-driven growth. As a result, we now have an economy that is fundamentally both debt-saturated and short of demand. Increasing economic inequality and exclusion was an inevitable corollary of this, as it had been in the 20s and 30s prior to the New Deal and World

War II. In fact, the weakness of aggregate demand actually *necessitated* low interest rates and asset price increases to keep the economy going (and this remains the case).[14]

On this reading, the only way to get the economy back on track is to restore the link between wage growth and productivity growth. As IMF economists wrote in 2010:

> *Without the prospect of a recovery in the incomes of poor and middle income households over a reasonable time horizon, the inevitable result is that loans keep growing, and therefore so does leverage and the probability of a major crisis that, in the real world, typically also has severe implications for the real economy.* (Kumhof & Ranciere, 2010: 22)

This would mean controlling corporate globalisation through labour and environmental standards that produce 'upward harmonisation' instead of the 'race to the bottom' (e.g., in corporate tax rates), as well as managed exchange rates; strengthening the ability of governments to produce public goods such as social security, health, education, and law and order; re-establishing full employment as the topmost goal of economic policy; strengthening the regulation of financial markets, going well beyond what had so far been done; reforming corporate governance so that companies were run in the interests of all their stakeholders, and not just their owners or managers; and reforming labour markets so that they provided good quality jobs paying reasonable wages that grew with productivity. This in turn meant reviving the trade unions so that workers can bargain effectively for a share of productivity gains; implementing a proper living wage to provide a true wage floor; and increasing worker protections and social security so that workers have the confidence to press their wage claims and exercise their rights as workers. There would also need to be greater redistribution of wealth through the tax system.

Some of these ideas have been progressed. For instance, Britain now has a higher national minimum wage, albeit one weakly enforced and still not a true living wage. The IMF (no less) has come out in favour of higher taxes for the better off (Georgieva, 2020) as has the OECD (2021). President Biden has taken a lead on corporate tax rates (Aldrick, 2021). And there is more openness to the use of fiscal policy to rebuild demand (Greeley, 2020; Wolf, 2020). Moreover, both Britain and America are now seeing robust wage growth on the back of Covid.

But there still seems to be more concern among economic policy makers and commentators about a long-term resurgence of inflation than about the damage that the long period of economic stagnation has done to our society. And the underlying imbalance between supply and demand has not changed, and indeed has been made even worse by Brexit and Covid, both of which will depress demand, at least in the short term if not for longer (Strauss, 2020). Moreover, by virtue of the fact that both bear most heavily on the less well-off, they will actually sharpen the differentials that were a major cause of the demand problem in the first place (Hall & Taylor, 2020).

3.3   Conclusion

In this chapter we looked at the impact of Neoliberalism on social and economic policy with a focus on socioeconomic inequality and economic growth. We found that over the period in which Neoliberal policies had been applied in Britain and America, inequality has risen, economic growth has slowed and economic instability has increased. In Chaps. 4 and 5 we consider some of the explanations given for the Neoliberal Turn.

Notes

1. As measured by the Gini coefficient, of the Organisation for Economic Cooperation and Development (OECD) and its Associates, only South Africa, Costa Rica, Chile, Mexico, Bulgaria and Turkey have higher levels of income inequality than the US and UK (retrieved 7 March 2022 from data.oecd.org/inequality/income-inequality.htm). The Gini coefficient measures inequality across the whole of a society rather than simply comparing different income groups.
2. Saez estimates that the top 1% of American families captured 45% of total real income growth per family from 2009 to 2018. In both countries there are even greater differentials within the top 1%.
3. Alstadsaeter et al. (2018) estimate that between 30 and 40% of all the wealth of the top 0.1% of UK households is owned abroad.
4. For global trends in inequality, see Piketty (2014 and 2020), Milanovic (2016) and World Inequality Lab (2022). Looking at a panel of 25 countries since 1970, Giovannoni (2010) found that both inequality and the overall wage share exhibited a turning point in the early 1980s (or 1990s, for some countries), that the pattern of poverty was closely related to the pattern of inequality and that these changes reflected 'the widespread

structural changes in institutions and economic policies since the start of the 1980s.

5. The Washington Consensus is the term used for the espousal of broadly Neoliberal policies over most of the post-1980s period by the major international intergovernmental organisations: the International Monetary Fund, the World Bank, the OECD, the European Union and, not least, the US Treasury (Irwin & Ward, 2021).

6. Krippner (2011) defines financialisation as profit-making through financial channels rather than through the supply of goods or services, with financial firms generating a disproportionate share of corporate profits (and political power). This has occurred as a result of the deregulation of financial markets, increased inflows of foreign capital to finance persistent deficits in countries like Britain and America, and heavy reliance on monetary measures for balancing the economy (see also Davis, 2009; Foroohar, 2016). Sharma (2021) estimates that since the 1970s the size of financial markets has exploded from about the same size as the global economy to four times the size, with most of the gains going to the wealthy as the main owners of financial assets. Duncan Weldon (2022) has recently argued that it was Britain's heavy reliance on its financial sector that—together with the Coalition Government's austerity policies—meant that our recovery from the finance-driven 2008–9 economic crisis was the weakest among the major advanced economies.

7. Lansley (2022: 183) states that 'in the UK 85% of the media in 2012 was owned by a handful of billionaires, with all of their companies registered abroad, thus paying little or no tax'.

8. In an article in *The Observer* in December 2020, two experts on modern British Government, Anand Menon and Jill Rutter, wrote that whilst the Brexit vote was a product of many factors:

   Most important of all, it resulted from the nature of our politics – adversarial, intolerant of compromise and pushing politicians to more extreme positions than the voters who put them there. That, above all, is cause for concern.

   Prasad's work is discussed further in Chap. 5. For the enhanced pursuit of status under Neoliberalism, see Storr (2021).

9. We should also note recent US work suggesting that increased inequality has played an important part in making America by far the most heavily polarised of the wealthy established democracies (Edsall, 2022).

10. There is no comparable body of work for Britain, but one of the emerging findings of the Institute of Fiscal Studies Deaton Review is that significant inequalities between firms are also common here (De Loecker et al., 2022).

11. The Bill provides that only Covid loans above £500,000 are to be published whereas under the EU rules in force up to the end of 2020 all loans over £100,000 were to be published.
12. Between 1960 and 1980, average annual growth in per capita GDP in constant (2015) US dollars for the OECD countries was 3%; for 1980–2019, it was 1.6% (Richard Upson, personal communication to the author).
13. Under quantitative easing, central banks buy government bonds from banks and investors, thereby releasing money and liquidity into the economy. However, it is now generally recognised that looser monetary conditions—not only quantitative easing but also lower interest rates—have been more effective in stimulating the financial markets than the economy, to the benefit of assetholders rather than wage earners, so further increasing inequality. In an article in the *New Statesman* in May 2022, Gary Stevenson estimated that most of the £450bn printed by the Bank of England in 2020 and 2021 had ended up in rich individuals' bank accounts.
14. For the full argument, see Stockhammer (2013). The Chancellor's (George Osborne's) strenuous efforts to stimulate the housing market—starting with Funding for Lending in 2012 and continuing with Help to Buy and changes in Stamp Duty that meant nearly all buyers paying less, and a more liberal (i.e., regressive) Inheritance Tax regime—were all classic instances of attempts to boost demand by such means (as well as retain the allegiance of better off voters). The cross-party House of Lords Built Environment Committee concluded (January 2022) that the £29bn spent on Help to Buy had increased prices but without improving supply. Rising house prices spread inequality as high rents and property values leave people who have to work without the means to buy all the production they are engaged in. In a 2014 paper, Professor John Muellbauer of the Oxford Economics Department showed how housing policy failures in the UK had widened intergenerational inequality, increased social exclusion, damaged productivity and growth, and raised the risk of financial instability. The Government does not appear to have learned much from these failures (Wolf, 2021).

REFERENCES

Aldrick, P. (2021, May 26). Sunak holds cards in Biden's tax plan talks. *The Times*.
Alstadsaeter, A., Johannesen, N., & Zucman, G. (2018). Who owns the wealth in tax havens? Macro evidence and implications for global inequality. *Journal of Public Economics, 162*, 89–100.
Atkinson, A. B., Piketty, Y., & Saez, E. (2011). Top incomes in the long run of history. *Journal of Economic Literature, 49*(1), 3–71.
Azmanova, A. (2019). *Capitalism on edge*. Columbia University Press.

BBC. (2021, March 24). *'Greed' and 'capitalism' helped UK's vaccines success, says PM.* Retrieved May 20, 2021, from https://www.bbc.co.uk/news/uk-politics-58504546

Brown, R. (2017). *The inequality crisis: What are the facts and what we can do about it.* Policy Press.

Caddick, D., & Stirling, A. (2021). *Half of UK families are £110 worse off a year since 2019 general election.* New Economics Foundation.

Chancel, L. (2017). *Unsustainable inequalities: Social justice and the environment.* Harvard University Press.

Dabla-Norris, E., Kochhar, K., Suphaphiphat, N., Ricka, F., & Tsounta, E. (2015). *Causes and consequences of income inequality: A global perspective.* IMF Staff Discussion Note SDN/15/13. International Monetary Fund.

Davis, G. F. (2009). *Managed by the markets: How finance reshaped America.* Oxford University Press.

De Loecker, J., Obermeier, T., & Van Reenen, J. (2022). *Firms and inequality. IFS deaton review of inequalities.* https://ifs.org.uk/inequality/firms-and-inequality.

Deaton, A. (2015). *The great escape: Health, wealth and the origins of inequality.* Princeton University Press.

Dorling, D. (2018). *Peak inequality: Britain's ticking time bomb.* Policy Press.

Edsall, T. (2022, January 26). America has split, and it's now in 'very dangerous territory'. *The New York Times.* Retrieved January 27, 2022, from https://www.nytimes.com/2022/01/26/opinion/covid-biden-trump-polarization.html.

Farnsworth, K. (2015). *The British corporate welfare state: Public provisions for private businesses.* Sheffield Political Economy Research Institute Paper No. 24. University of Sheffield.

Federal Reserve. (2021). *DFA: Distributional financial accounts distribution of household wealth in the U.S. since 1989.*

Fleming, S. (2017, November 28). US tax reform: the return of trickle-down economics. *Financial Times.* Retrieved November 28, 2017, from https://www.ft.com/content/8b5233a6-d142-11e7-9dbb-291a884dd8c6.

Foroohar, R. (2016). *Makers and takers: The rise of finance and the fall of American business.* Crown Business.

Foroohar, R. (2020, September 28). Concentrated power in Big Tech harms the US. *Financial Times.* Retrieved January 12, 2021, from https://www.ft.com/content/06ad9abe-73aa-44f7-b1fe-08dc16854610.

Frank, R. H., & Cook, P. J. (2010). *The winner-take-all-society: Why the few at the top get so much more.* Virgin.

Furman, J., & Orszag, P. (2015). *A firm-level perspective on the role of rents in the rise in inequality.* Retrieved March 2, 2022, from https://Gabriel-zucman.eu/files/teaching/FurmanOrszag.pdf.

Georgieva, K. (2020 January 7). *Reduce inequality to create opportunity*. Retrieved January 8, 2020, from https://blogs.imf.org/2020/01/07/reduce-inequality-to-create-opportunity.

Giovannoni, O. (2010). *Functional distribution of income, inequality and the incidence of poverty: Stylized facts and the role of macroeconomic policy*. University of Texas Inequality Project Working Paper No. 58.

Greeley, B. (2020, January 7). Economists fear US is approaching limit of monetary policy. *Financial Times*. https://www.ft.com/content/e82bfb10-3136-11ea-a329-0bcf87a328f2.

Hall, P., & Taylor, R. (2020, June 22). Pandemic deepens social and political cleavages. *Social Europe*. Retrieved February 1, 2021, from https://www.socialeurope.eu/pandemic-deepens-social-and-political-cleavages.

Hills, J., McKnight, A., & Bucelli, I. (2019). *Understanding the relationship between poverty and inequality*. Centre for Analysis of Social Exclusion, London School of Economics.

Irwin, D., & Ward, O. (2021, September 8). *What is the "Washington Consensus?"* Peterson Institute for International Economics. Retrieved February 7, 2022, from https://www.piie.com/blogs/realtime-economic-issues-watch/what-washington-consensus.

Johnson, B. (2013). *What would Maggie do today?* Boris Johnson's speech at the Margaret Thatcher lecture in full. Retrieved March 3, 2022, from http://www.telegraph.co.uk/news/politics/london-mayor-election-mayor-of-london/10480321/Boris-Johnsons-speech-at-the-Margaret-Thatcher-lecture-in-full.html.

Joseph, K. (1976). *Stranded on the middle ground?* Centre for Policy Studies.

Klein, M. C., & Pettis, M. (2020). *Trade wars are class wars: How rising inequality distorts the global economy and threatens international peace*. Yale University Press.

Krippner, G. R. (2011). *Capitalizing on crisis: The political origins of the rise of finance*. Harvard University Press.

Kumhof, M., & Ranciere, R. (2010). *Inequality, leverage and crises*. IMF Working Paper WP/10/268. International Monetary Fund.

Kuttner, R. (2018). *Can democracy survive global capitalism?* W.W.Norton.

Lansley, S. (2022). *The richer, the poorer: How Britain enriched the few and failed the poor*. Policy Press.

Lazo-Gonzalez, D. (2019). The dance of those left over. In *The Oxford magazine. Fifth week* (pp. 14–15). Michaelmas Term.

Lindsey, B., & Teles, S. M. (2019). *The captured economy: How the powerful enrich themselves, slow down growth, and increase inequality*. Viking.

Lynn, B. C. (2021, July/August). Antimonopoly power: The global fight against corporate concentration. *Foreign Affairs*.

MacLean, N. (2017). *Democracy in chains: The deep history of the radical right's stealth plan for America*. Scribe.

Marmot, M. (2015). *The health gap: The challenge of an unequal world*. Bloomsbury.

Milanovic, B. (2016). *Global inequality: A new approach for the age of globalization*. Belknap Press of Harvard University Press.

Nixon, S. (2022, February 10). The reality of Brexit appears to be protectionism and secret subsidies. *The Times*.

OECD. (2021). *Inheritance Taxation in OECD Countries*. OECD.

Office for National Statistics. (2021a, January 21). *Household income inequality, UK: financial year ending 2020*.

Office for National Statistics. (2021b, November 10). *Labour costs and labour income*.

Office for National Statistics. (2022, January 7). *Household total wealth in Great Britain: April 2018 to March 2020*.

Oswald, Y., Owen, A., & Steinberger, J. K. (2020). Large inequality in international and intranational energy footprints between income groups and across consumption categories. *Nature Energy, 5*, 231–239. Retrieved January 13, 2021, from https://doi.org/10.1038/s41560-020-0579-8.

Palley, T. I. (2012). *From financial crisis to stagnation: The destruction of shared prosperity and the role of economics*. Cambridge University Press.

Phillipon, T. (2019). *The great reversal: How America gave up on free markets*. Harvard University Press.

Piketty, T. (2014). *Capital in the twenty-first century*. Harvard University Press.

Piketty, T. (2020). *Capital and ideology*. The Belknap Press of Harvard University Press.

Prasad, M. (2006). *The politics of free markets*. University of Chicago Press.

Saez, E. (2020). *Striking it richer: The evolution of top incomes in the United States (Updated with 2018 estimates)*. UC Berkeley. https://eml.berkeley.edu/~saez/saez-UStopincomes-2018.pdf.

Shambaugh, J., Nunn, R., Breitweiser, A., & Liu, P. (2018) *The state of competition and dynamism: Facts about concentration, start-ups, and related policies*. Retrieved June 13, 2018, from hamiltonproject.org/papers/the_state_of_competition_and_dynamism_facts_about_concentration_start_

Sharma, R. (2021, January 20). Dear Joe Biden, deficits still matter. *Financial Times*. Retrieved January 20, 2021, from https://www.ft.com/content/d49b537a-95f8-4e1a-b4b1-19f0c44d751e

St Louis Fed. (2021, January 21). *Share of labour compensation in GDP at current national prices for United States*. Retrieved February 2, 2022, from https://fred.stlouisfed.org/series/LABSHPUSA156NRUG.

Stevenson, G. (2022, 25 May). The UK government gave £450bn to the richest – should take it back for the people. *New Statesman*.

Stockhammer, E. (2013). Why have wage shares fallen? An Analysis of the determinants of functional income distribution. In M. Lavoie & E. Stockhammer (Eds.), *Wage-led growth: An equitable strategy for economic recovery* (pp. 40–70). Palgrave Macmillan.

Strauss, D. (2020, October 7). Hidden joblessness threatens economic recovery in US and Europe. *Financial Times*. https://www.ft.com/content/ec3d88dc-0dc1-4f6e-adf7-37e8f4316a22.

Summers, L. (2013, November 8). *Transcript of Larry summers speech at the IMF economic forum*. Retrieved November 19, 2014, from http://www.facebook.com/notes/randy-fellmy/transcript-of-larry-summers-speech-at-the-imf-economic-forum-nov-8-2013/585630634864563.

Summers, L. (2017, November 6). A Republican tax plan that will help the rich and harm growth. *Financial Times*. Retrieved November 6, 2017, from https://www.ft.com/content/5c0be71a-bf2a-11e7-823b-ed31693349d3.

Storr, W. (2021). *The status game: On social status and how we use it*. William Collins.

Tepper, J., & Hearn, D. (2019). *The myth of capitalism: Monopolies and the death of competition*. Wiley.

United Nations Environment Programme. (2020). *Emissions gap report 2020*. Retrieved January 14, 2021, from https://www.unep.org/emissions-gap-report-2020.

Weldon, D. (2022, 17–23 June). The new sick man of Europe. *New Statesman*.

Wilkinson, R., & Pickett, K. (2009). *The spirit level: Why equal societies almost always do better*. Allen Lane.

Wilkinson, R., & Pickett, K. (2018). *The inner level*. Allen Lane.

Wolf, M. (2014, September 30). Why inequality is such a drag on economics. *Financial Times* Retrieved January 15, 2021, from ft.com/content/8b41dfc8-47c1-11e4-ac9f-00144feab7de.

Wolf, M. (2020, November 30). Weak demand would derail Britain's economic comeback. *Financial Times*. Retrieved November 20, 2020, from https://www.ft.com/content/973609ef-9a26-46cc-a9ad-32c2f69fe8d9.

Wolf, M. (2021, March 21). British housing is expensive and its supply must increase. *Financial Times*. Retrieved December 17, 2021, from https://www.ft.com/content/75942d5f-6bdf-40fb-b7ce-a48429ab84fc.

World Inequality Lab. (2022). *World inequality report 2022*. https://wir2022.wid.world/.

Zucman, G. (2016). *The hidden wealth of nations*. Chicago University Press.

CHAPTER 4

Explaining the Neoliberal Turn: Structural Theories

Abstract The consideration in Chap. 3 of the damaging impact of Neoliberal social and economic policies on inequality and economic growth inevitably prompts the question of why the Neoliberal Turn occurred in the first place. Once again we distinguish between structural theories that draw attention to underlying, longer-term factors often bound up with the nature of capitalism and institutional theories that emphasise the role of political actors, institutions and cultures. This chapter deals mostly with the structural theories, and Chap. 5 with the institutional ones. The former are considered under the following headings: the retreat from Keynesianism; the power of ideas; the shock doctrine; financialisation; the globalisation of finance; the capitalists' revolt; Keynesianism, Monetarism and the crisis of the state; and the crises of capitalism.

Keywords Capitalism • Financialisation • Globalisation • Keynesianism • Monetarism • Neoliberalism

> *The energy crisis caught us with our parameters down. The food crisis caught us too. This was a year of infamy in inflation forecasting. There are many things we really just don't know* (Walter Heller, noted Keynesian economist and former Chairman of the President's

Council of Economic Advisers, reported in the *New York Times*, 29
December 1973, quoted in Stein, *2010*: 118).

4.1   The Retreat from Keynesianism

Colin Crouch attributed the Neoliberal Turn to what he termed the
'Achilles heel' of Keynesianism: 'the inflationary tendencies of its politically determined ratchet' (Crouch, 2011: 13). Faced by inflation, workers
bid up their wages, but governments responded only slowly, by cutting
expenditure and/or raising taxes. This defect of demand management was
exposed by the commodity price rises of the 1970s, especially the two oil
price hikes. As a result,

> *Governments could not be trusted to put the soundness of the economy ahead of
> short-term popularity by risking interventions that weakened the ability of the
> market to do its work of rewarding success, punishing failure and allowing
> consumers to make choices* (Crouch, 2011: 14–15).

The defeat of Keynesianism was assisted by the decline of the industrial
working classes. Rising productivity and the globalisation of production
meant that the share of employment accounted for by mining and manufacturing was in decline. The traditional unions were therefore less effective whilst workers in the newer areas of the economy—services and
especially financial services—were much less organised. The remaining
areas of heavily unionised employment were mostly in the public sector
and the Government was able to deal with these directly (as when President
Reagan took on the air traffic controllers and Mrs. Thatcher the miners).
A further factor was the availability of a body of theory—the Chicago
school of economists, building on Hayek and Von Mises—that vindicated
the new approach.

Even so, by the early 1980s the instability inherent in Neoliberalism
was beginning to become apparent. But

> *two very different forces* [then] *came together to rescue the Neoliberal model …
> the growth of credit markets for poor and middle-income people, and the emer-
> gence of derivatives and futures markets among the very wealthy. This combi-
> nation produced a model of "privatized Keynesianism" that occurred initially
> by chance, but which gradually became a crucial matter for public policy.
> Instead of governments taking on debt to stimulate the economy, individuals*

and families did so, including some rather poor ones (Crouch, 2011:114; see also Crouch, 2009 and Lansley, 2011).

As well as the wealthy, the principal beneficiaries of the Neoliberal Turn were large corporations (cf. Reich, 2016). This is ironic because such firms often represent a concentration of economic power that is or should be anathema to market purists. Another irony is that the despised state is still required to create or maintain the conditions for markets and firms to function (e.g., the bank bailouts in 2008–09 and, more recently, the Covid support measures).[1]

4.2   THE POWER OF IDEAS

Mark Blyth (2002) identified the late-1960s/early 1970s as the second major breakdown in the capitalist economy in the twentieth century, the first being the Depression of the 1930s that led to Polanyi's (1944) 'Great Transformation'.[2] In such situations, ideas reduce the uncertainty inherent in such crises. They enable collective action and coalition-building. They are an essential resource for attacking and restructuring institutions. Once those institutions are delegitimised, the new ideas serve as blueprints for replacements. Finally, the same ideas enable institutional stability by generating conventions that make the institutional coordination of agents' expectations possible.

Blyth illustrates this thesis by describing in considerable detail how in both the US and Sweden the earlier crisis saw the creation of 'embedded Liberalism' (Ruggie, 1982) while the later crisis saw its demise (although in essence Neoliberalism was a throwback to the classical economic theories that were refuted by Keynes).

In the US, the Depression discredited the classically derived policies of sound finance and fiscal orthodoxy. This led to stronger state action to empower labour and the unions and enhance social security and pensions, on the basis that industrial labour was the key to remedying underconsumption ('stagnationism'). The need to mobilise for war, and the involvement of many businessmen in the war effort, also legitimised the leadership role of the state. Yet the power of business and the normal Jeffersonian animus against government meant that whilst action to stabilise the economy was acceptable, anything that smacked of redistribution was out (a policy known as 'growthmanship', the idea being that growth would secure whatever redistribution was needed).

In Sweden, the hold of embedded liberalism was less tenuous. It owed a good deal to the early ascendancy of the Swedish Democratic Party. After a classical start, the Party's progressive economic thinking owed much to the Stockholm School of economists who were well ahead of their American contemporaries. What emerged was a compromise whereby the underlying idea was the expansion of the whole economy—15 years before the US—with price stability as the core objective combined with an ambitious programme of public works. Business was accommodated through taxes that encouraged investment and policies that promoted industrial concentration. After the war, and again unlike the US, the labour unions continued to lead economic thinking with profit-capping, a 'solidarity' (minimum) wage and active labour market policies. Finally, the new white-collar workers were bound into state pension arrangements.

Blyth attributed the unseating of embedded liberalism in the US to a combination of state failures—the control of the inflation that stemmed from the Vietnam War, the cost of the Great Society reforms, the 1971 closing of the gold window by President Nixon (see Chap. 5) and, later, the first oil shock—and business discomfort at the extension of state power through enhanced regulation and price controls, even under Republican Presidents (increased civil and labour unrest may also have played a part):

The combined effect of these policy failures was to signal to business that the state had expanded its role well beyond the limits established as reasonable in the 1940s and 1950s. Consequently, business reacted against these infringements on what it saw as its fundamental rights and sought to replace the embedded liberal order with one more attuned to its interests, at least as business interpreted them in this highly uncertain environment. (Blyth, 2002: 139)

This remobilisation of business was greatly assisted by the effective removal of limits on political donations (the 1971 Campaign Finance Reform Act and the 1975 SUNPAC judgement).

Not only Republican but also Democrat politicians—beginning with Jimmy Carter's acceptance, for the purposes of winning the 1976 election campaign, that 'deficits cause inflation'—were gradually won over to supply-side thinking. Institutionally, embedded liberalism was doomed by Congressional unwillingness to sanction tax increases and by the Fed's commitment to Monetarism (these in turn reflecting the historical weakness of American central government other than in war or a major crisis). Unfortunately, the one alternative developed by the

Democrats—industrial policy—was hard to launch, and anyway was still within the Neoliberal frame.

4.3   The Shock Doctrine

Naomi Klein coined the term 'the shock doctrine' to describe,

> *the quite brutal tactic of systematically using the public's disorientation follow-ing a collective shock – wars, coups, terrorist attacks, market crashes, or natural disasters – to push through radical pro-corporate measures, often called "shock therapy".* (Klein, N. 2017: 2)

Klein applied this to the Trump administration's attempt to capitalise on the after-shocks of the 2008–09 crisis. But the basic idea—of exploiting the gap between events and our initial ability to explain them—could also be applied to the conservative response to the inflationary surges of the 1970s (and even perhaps to the Vietnam War and its impact on America). Like Crouch, Reich and others, Klein sees major corporations as the major beneficiaries of the recent crisis.

4.4   Financialisation

Daniel Bell (1978) argued that as a result of the additional responsibilities taken on by the state during the first half of the twentieth century—for the direction of the economy, support for research and innovation, the redressing of economic and social inequalities—it faced an inescapable dilemma between (a) creating or maintaining the conditions in which the necessary profitable capital accumulation can occur, and (b) maintaining the social harmony needed for the capital accumulation (cf. Rose & Peters, 1978).

Building on Bell, Greta R. Krippner (2011) argued that financialisation had been a means of avoiding the allocative choices posed by the slowdown in postwar economic growth in the 1970s: crudely, who should bear the burden of a fading prosperity? The key mechanisms were the removal of controls limiting the rates of interest that could be paid on savings deposits (in 1980, under President Carter) and the expansion of credit (during the 1970s).[3]

In fact, financialisation was a response to three related crises: social (slowing growth made the conflicts between different groups sharper); fiscal (increasing pressures on the state to provide services to support economic growth that outstripped its capacity to generate revenues, not helped by the costs of the Vietnam War) and legitimacy (the first two crises led to a loss of confidence in the state to sustain economic growth and support social objectives). The response was inadvertent, rather than the deliberate or planned outcome sought by policymakers.

In a similar vein, Gerald Davis (2009) argued that the financial markets had reshaped the transition from an industrial to a post-industrial economy. By the early twentieth century, the large, vertically integrated industrial corporation had become the key organising structure for economic and social life, exerting a 'gravitational pull' on society. But this role had now fallen to financial markets and services. This reflected the combined effects of globalisation and technology which had changed both the kinds of things that can be produced (with a pronounced shift to 'intangibles') and the cost profile of different organisational arrangements. The consequent gains in productivity meant that fewer workers were needed.

Financialisation had also undermined the commercial banks. Losing their privileged access to information, they moved away from taking deposits and lending to fee-based services, investment banking and other activities (even as greater conflicts of interest were created), in the process yielding ground and influence to investment banks and mutuals. At the same time, the 'efficient market hypothesis' provided a rationale for the conversion of the corporation from a tangible organisation with members, obligations and sovereign boundaries to a nexus of contracts devoted to 'shareholder value'.[4] The key development here was the hostile takeover boom of the 1980s.

What had happened to companies was mirrored in what had happened to the state. States changed from being sovereign authorities to vendors of business services, especially the protection of intellectual property but also law more generally (often in competition with other states). In the same process, outsourcing and sub-contracting had hollowed out the state's resources and expertise (as we have seen in the UK Government's initial response to the Covid crisis: see Chap. 7).

Finally, just like corporations, individuals had been encouraged to think of their job as a setting for enhancing their 'human capital' while their financial capital accumulates. Through both direct ownership of shares but also indirect ownership through mutual funds, workers had come to have a share in the ownership society (and become good Republicans). Individuals were in effect investors in their own capital. What we had in fact was the 'portfolio society' where nearly everything can be seen as an investment (as in the UK higher education reforms described in Chap. 2). The paradox is that whilst the US economy had never been more productive, Americans had never felt more insecure. There were five main problems: less social mobility, more inequality; educational uncertainty; the end of the corporate safety net (health insurance, some measure of retirement security); dangerous financial services affecting not just the contracting parties and a 'brain drain' from Government to contractors (cf. Foroohar, 2016).

4.5   The Globalisation of Finance

Eric Helleiner (1994) charted the progressive globalisation of finance between 1944 and the early 1990s. The 1944 Bretton Woods agreement that states could and should control capital movements and interest rates, and with the dollar linked to gold, was in part a response to the chaos that followed the collapse of the Gold Standard in 1931, and in part a reflection of the 'embedded Liberal' position of many officials, academics and industrialists that such controls were necessary to prevent the new interventionist welfare state from being undermined by speculative and disequilibriating cross-border capital flows.

However, the agreement was undermined by four main sets of factors: its vulnerability to unilateral liberalisation by individual states; the loss of support from the US (needing help to fund its deficits but wanting to retain policy autonomy) and the UK (seeking to preserve London's position as a major international finance centre), and later Japan; the increasing strength of the Neoliberal position in economic thinking; and the survival of the Bank for International Settlements as a vehicle for cooperation between the central banks.

While the process was gradual, the Thatcher Government's abolition of exchange controls in 1979 and the Fed's decision in 1981 to permit the establishment of tax-free international banking facilities on US soil were crucial steps (the US had abolished capital controls in 1974). Indeed, Helleiner stressed the key role in the process played by states and their governments, and the central part played in particular by the US. States were vital not only in allowing and then promoting liberalisation but also—through acting as 'lender of last resort' and more closely supervising the banks—in successfully defusing the 1974 banking crisis, the 1982 debt crisis and the 1987 stock market fall (as of course they did in 2008–09).

Ann Pettifor (2006) went further back than Helleiner. From 1944 to 1971 the Bretton Woods system, although under increasing pressure, provided a measure of international financial stability. It was brought to an end by the August 1971 decision that the dollar would no longer be linked to gold, nor would payments be made in gold (see Chap. 5). Instead of paying its debts by selling exports and earning gold (with which to pay its creditors), the US offered its creditors bank money in the form of debt (Treasury bills). This began the removal of controls over the international movement of capital:

> The US could expect to borrow money in the currency it printed. By revaluing or devaluing that currency the US could, therefore, increase or lower the value of its foreign debts. Furthermore, because there was no longer any benchmark (i.e., gold) against which its currency would be measured, or indeed any constraints against which its balances (imports/exports) would be assessed, the US need never again be obliged to **structurally adjust** its economy to restore it to balance (a requirement regularly made, since the 1980s, of poor, debtor nations). This meant that the US could now borrow limitless amounts of money on the international capital markets without restraint, and use these resources to pursue apparently endless consumption. (Pettifor, 2006: 42, original author's emphases)

The consequences for the US, for the international economy and within national economies and democracies, were profound. The US had massively increased consumption and moved from being the world's biggest creditor to being the world's biggest debtor. Financial liberalisation had fostered global imbalances, deficits and debts, fraud and corruption, and international financial crises. There had also been an international transfer of wealth as money moved from where it is scarce (low-income countries like China and India with large numbers of poor) to where it is plentiful (high-income countries like the US and UK). Finally, the post-1971 global financial system had also increased inequalities *within* countries. Those who own assets have seen the value of those assets become inflated while everyone else found their wages, commodities and other prices falling, or deflating, as a share of the whole economy. Globalisation also puts many workers in high-income countries into competition with workers in low-income ones.

To summarise:

Today's liberalized international financial and trading system differs only in scale from the divisive and unstable international system of the gold standard. Globalization is a system characterized by high real rates of interest, low investment, high unemployment, low wages and high rates of debt. It is a system that has generated an embarrassment of riches for the rich, and which shrinks the share of the global economic cake allocated to workers, and those who do not own assets. Above all it is a system that prioritizes the interests of international creditors – as it did under the gold standard (Pettifor, 2006: 51).

At the same time:

Elected democratic governments have been weakened, and lack the powers, resources and institutions to protect their citizens and firms and to compensate citizens when shocks occur, for example to pension funds. In some countries the failure of government to afford protection to citizens is leading to disillusionment with spineless parliaments; and with leaders that have given away to invisible 'markets' key powers to allocate resources – for health, public sanitation, transport etc. These markets are failing to provide pensions, hospitals, railways, schools and culture to the satisfaction of their communities. As a result, there is growing disillusionment with the democratic process (Pettifor, 2006: 52).

We shall come back to these issues in Chaps. 6 and 7.[5]

4.6   THE CAPITALISTS' REVOLT

Wolfgang Streeck (2017) also starts with Daniel Bell's tension between capital accumulation and the conditions necessary for it, notably popular support that would legitimate it:

Capitalism is about the expansion of expandable property in the form of private property; this entails the danger of a withdrawal of cooperation by those who are needed for accumulation but will not own what is accumulated. (Streeck, 2017: xix)

In the postwar period this cooperation was achieved through a mixed economy in which the state played a key role in balancing the interests of capital and labour: 'socially controlled capitalism'. But

> *beginning in the early 1980s, central elements of the social contract of postwar capitalism were gradually revoked or called into question in the societies of the West: politically guaranteed full employment, collective society-wide wage formation negotiated with free trade unions, worker participation at workplace and enterprise level, state control of key industries, a broad public sector with secure employment as a model for the private sector, universal social rights protected from competition, tax and income policies that kept inequality within tight limits, and government cyclical and industrial policies to secure steady growth.* (Streeck, 2017: 28)

With the slowdown in growth in the late 1960s and the demand of the wage-dependent (as in the 1968 strikes) that they should continue to enjoy job security and welfare protection, the profit-dependent owners and managers of capital took fright at the risk of a profits squeeze. The energy crisis of the early and mid-1970s was another important factor. So there was indeed a crisis of legitimation. But it was not the risk of the loss of *worker* support (that had traditionally concerned theorists), but the threat of *capitalist* withdrawal of support from a regime that they had had to endorse as part of postwar reconstruction.

The main form which this withdrawal of capitalist support took, and the main cause of lower growth and higher unemployment, was a withdrawal of investment. These owners also pushed for market deregulation (not only of labour markets and not only within domestic economies) and tax cuts. Their 'weapons' included temporarily laying idle the resources allocated to them by society as 'property' and completely moving these out of the country (for which the increased mobility of persons and capital through globalisation was helpful); 'massive uncertainty' was another familiar trope. At the same time, the state role was progressively reduced to providing for the functioning and regulation of markets.

Postwar capitalism, and especially consumption, was sustained (and distributional conflicts avoided or postponed) through a number of mechanisms, each of which had to do with money (here there is some common ground with Krippner). Now the only money left with which to secure continuing mass allegiance to the capitalist model and the illusion of growth and prosperity was the fiat money of the central banks (in purchasing public debt and bank liabilities—quantitative easing), and even this was hardly shifting the growth curve (whilst having serious distributional side effects as it increases the value of financial assets, as already noted).

So what started as the 'tax state' became the 'debt state' (where the state had to borrow moneys that it should have raised through taxes, from companies and the wealthy), and is now the 'consolidation state', committed to fiscal consolidation and austerity. With this third phase, power has shifted to the central banks, which more than ever have become the real governments of post-democratic capitalism, insulated from voters, trade unions, parliaments, governments, etc., like no other public institution. But

keeping capitalism going by expanding the balance sheets of central banks cannot continue forever: once again, what starts out as a solution sooner or later turns into a problem. (Streeck, 2017: xxxix)

Hence the successive, and so far unsuccessful, attempts to 'end the ride on the tiger' of quantitative easing. In fact,

the money magic of the past two decades, produced with the help of an unfettered finance industry, may have finally become too dangerous for governments to dare to buy more time with it. (Streeck, 2017: xxxiv)

Indeed, in spite of all attempts to conjure them away,

*the three trends that mark the gradual decay of present-day capitalism as a socio-economic order ... are continuing unabated, and in fact seem to have begun to reinforce each other in a downward spiral: **declining growth**, **increasing inequality** and rising **overall debt** – low growth resulting in more unequal distribution, with increasing concentration of wealth among the top '1 per cent' in turn standing in the way of higher growth; economic stagnation making debt reduction more difficult, just as high debt inhibits the new credit required for new growth, even at rock-bottom interest rates; and ever growing debt adding to the risk of a new collapse of the financial system.* (Streeck, 2017: xxxiv – xxxv, original author's emphases)[6]

As well as causing the weaker performance of most Western economies since the mid-1970s, the capitalists' revolt accounts for the growing popular disenchantment with conventional politics:

Political-economic conflict over distribution moved even further outside the experience of the man or woman in the street and their ability to influence it politically: that is, it gradually shifted from the usual wage struggle at enterprise level towards parliamentary elections, from there to private loan and insurance markets, and then to a realm of international financial diplomacy completely remote from everyday life, whose issues and strategies were a closed book for everyone except those directly involved, and perhaps even for them too. (Streeck, 2017: 46)

So far from making life harder for the capitalists (the familiar complaint of Neoliberal reformers), the real failure of postwar Western democracy has been to refrain from making the beneficiaries of capitalist economic growth pay the social costs of their gains. There is a paradox here:

With advancing economic and social development the collective expenditure required to facilitate [capital accumulation] *must increase – for example, for the repair of collateral damage (as after 2008), the installation and maintenance of an ever more demanding infrastructure, the creation of the necessary 'human capital', the underwriting of the required work and performance motivation,* etc. (Streeck, 2017: xx)

Yet, the same firms that seek better roads, airports, schools, research funding, etc., also want tax reductions and reliefs (as already noted). The result is that taxes on small and medium incomes rise—through higher consumption taxes and social security contributions—leading to an even more regressive tax system.

Another failure has been the almost complete unwillingness to discuss the distributive impact of the transition from the tax state to the debt state. The 'winners' in the struggle in the market and with the tax authorities

need a state that will not only leave them their money as private property but borrow it and keep it safe, pay interest on it and, last but not least, let them pass it on to their children – by virtue of inheritance taxes that have long been inconsequential. In this way the state as debt state serves to perpetuate extant patterns of stratification and the social inequality built into them. (Streeck, 2017: 78)

4.7   KEYNESIANISM, MONETARISM AND THE CRISIS OF THE STATE

Simon Clarke (1988) saw the espousal of Neoliberal ideas by such as Thatcher and Reagan as essentially providing a rationale for what they would have done anyway: 'monetarism is the ideological mask that seeks to conceal this capitalist counter-offensive' (1988: 6). Nor were Keynesianism and Monetarism ('the need to maintain monetary stability to ensure the smooth operation of the market and the achievement of a full employment equilibrium', 1988: 323) fundamentally opposed; indeed, he pointed to several areas of agreement between them. Clarke explained Monetarism's success as follows:

> *The strength of monetarism was ideological, for monetarism could articulate, in however mystified a form, growing popular opposition to the bureaucratic and authoritarian forms of the capitalist state, which the Labour Party had failed to mobilise politically, while providing a theory that could explain the failure of both Keynesianism and militant trades unionism, and legitimate the policies that had been forced on reluctant Keynesian governments. The ideological merit of the Conservatives' monetarism was that it made a virtue of necessity, representing these crisis measures as the core principles of a new ideology of state regulation. It was not so much its positive merits that gave monetarism its appeal, as the manifest failure of Keynesianism. This was articulated in Thatcher's triumphant refrain that 'there is no alternative'.* (1988: 329–30)

The central issue was whether the state exists to promote and protect capitalism or to work in the interests of the people as a whole (where those interests conflict): should the accumulation of capital be subordinated to the aspirations of the working classes?

On this reading, the 1970s crisis was essentially a crisis in the accumulation of capital:

> *Between the popular demand for rising incomes and employment, which could only be satisfied by the growth of production, and the capitalist need to subordinate production to profit.* [It was] *a structural crisis of accumulation.* (1988: 12)

This overproduction arose from a combination of greater efficiency through technological and managerial innovations, and larger markets through globalisation and the removal or lowering of trade barriers ('the massive internationalisation of productive capital'), on top of the resurgence of the continental European and Japanese economies after the war. However, the crisis was greater in some countries than in others. Where domestic productive capital was strong (as in Austria, Sweden and, to some extent, Germany), there was collaboration between the various interests. So that

> the working class as a whole could be reconciled to the intensification of labour and to substantial structural changes in employment through collaborative incomes policies, 'manpower planning', retraining schemes and generous welfare benefits, at least for so long as capital was able to confine the aspirations of the working class within the limits of profitability. However in Britain such institutions had been developed in response to a deterioration in collaborative class relations, marked by growing working class militancy and a fall in the profitability of domestic productive capital. (1988: 299)

Unfortunately, Britain suffered historically from weak domestic productive capital because of a low rate of investment which in turn reflected 'the ability … to retreat into the protected markets of the empire in the face of successive world crises' (1988: 292), something denied to Germany, the US and Japan. Nevertheless, these contradictions—between continuing profitability, on the one hand, and rising wages and public expenditure, on the other—were ultimately 'an expression of the contradictions of the capitalist state form as the growing pressure of overaccumulation overwhelmed the post-war settlement' (1988: 304).

Clarke noted that the skilled working class was ripe for Thatcherism:

> Rising public expenditure had meant that the incidence of taxation had moved progressively down the income scale, so that the welfare state brought a net advantage only to the lowest income earners, the mass of the working class benefitting more from cuts in taxation than from increases in public expenditure. (1988: 320)

They were also open to the assault on the trade unions which further weakened opposition to monetarist policies. (There are clear parallels here with the Republicans under Reagan.)

Clarke also noted that Monetarism 'certainly does not involve a withdrawal of the state in favour of the market' (p. 355). Nor does it entail a strengthening of democracy:

The increasingly ruthless subordination of civil society and the state to the power of money has ... led to the progressive erosion of the legitimacy of representative and democratic bodies, which are reduced to the fora within which particular interests press their partisan claims, and against which monetarism asserts the primacy of the general interest embodied in the disinterested rule of money. The authoritarianism of monetarist regimes is not a quirk of the personality of their political leaders, but is inherent in the monetarist project. (1988: 356)

Nevertheless, Monetarism had not removed the tendency to overaccumulation or confined it within the ambit of the market:

Indeed the sharpening of international competition and the rapid pace of technical change through the 1980s intensified the overaccumulation and uneven development of capital, which was accommodated only by the explosion of domestic and international debt. While the boom was sustained governments were able to isolate working class resistance to restrictive economic and social policies and aggressive managerial strategies, while capital was able to concede a steady rise in the wages of large sections of the working class. The political stability of monetarism, no less than that of Keynesianism, depended on the sustained, if uneven accumulation of capital on a world scale. (1988: 357)

So Monetarism was vulnerable to a worsening of international economic conditions, albeit in different ways to Keynesianism.

4.8   THE DEREGULATION OF FINANCE

Tomaskovic-Devey and Lin (2011) shared the general 'mobilisation of capital' thesis as leading to the installation of the Neoliberal model ('a series of state practices that favor market rather than regulatory or administrative solutions'):

In 1973, surges in oil prices increased the cost of manufacturing and transportation while transferring income to oil producing firms and countries. The rise in union and consumer power put real limits on corporate autonomy in the labor process and the market. Manufacturing competition from Japan and northern Europe ended the postwar era of U.S. global manufacturing hegemony. The resulting low-growth, high-inflation macro-economy undermined the legitimacy of Keynesian economic solutions. This configuration of threats led the large-firm corporate sector to mobilize to reinvent the system; they pushed for economic deregulations, lower taxes, and a smaller state (Harvey, 2005; Vogel 1989). (Tomaskovic-Devey & Lin, 2011: 542)

The authors focused on the role of financial institutions in exploiting the new policy climate. The stagflation of the early and mid-1970s reduced the income of banks and other financial entities. But the banks in particular benefitted from Paul Volcker's tightening of monetary conditions and from the rise in capital surpluses in OPEC and Europe, as well as the growth in institutional investors such as pension funds (on page 543 they quote an estimate that by 2008 the US accounted for nearly half the entire world's capital imports). But the biggest factor in financialisation had been deregulation.

This began with the 1978 Supreme Court ruling in *Marquette National Bank of Minneapolis v. First of Omaha Service Corporation* that credit card companies could charge the allowable interest rate in the state where they were chartered. But the key factor was the series of decisions that allowed the creation of cross-industry entities, which in turn led to increased concentration and the centrality of the largest financial institutions in the economy (the latter being reflected in much higher shares of corporate profits and employee compensation).

At the same time,

> *the finance conception of a firm as a bundle of tradeable assets replaced nonfinance sector managerial commitments to investment and innovation in specific markets* (Davis, 2009). *This shift led to a fundamental change in managerial behaviour. Finance-oriented managers now controlled major corporations, and short-term planning to increase stock prices became a primary managerial focus.* (Tomaskovic-Devey & Lin, 2011: 545)

The main result was an estimated transfer of between $5.8tn and 6.6tn to the finance sector since 1980. These income rents were realised primarily by capital (direct and indirect owners) in the banking, insurance and real estate sectors, and by employees (managerial, professional and service occupations) in the securities industry. The authors commented:

> *If neoliberalism is a policy and intellectual movement away from state regulation, financialization is perhaps its most fundamental product. Certainly, the transfer of national wealth into the finance sector is one of its most dramatic consequences.* (Tomaskovic-Devey & Lin, 2011: 556)

But whilst the market and political power of finance was crucial, we should not overlook other actors:

> *Consumers looking for interest rates better than inflation, institutional investors with cash to invest, corporate shareholders and CEOs seeking to maximize short-term profits for immediate rewards, and even the Federal Reserve Bank, attempting to obscure its political role in producing unemployment and slowing wage growth. While we do not dispute power's fundamental role in producing market rents, a great deal of idiosyncrasy is produced by multiple actors attempting to solve multiple problems as they arise in real historical time. Nonfinancial business elites and the state might have been the most commanding actors around 1980, but they gradually lost their dominance to the financial sector.* (Tomaskovic-Devey & Lin, 2011: 555)

4.9   THE CRISES OF CAPITALISM

The tension between capital accumulation and the social conditions necessary for it is one of the three 'conundrums' that Andrew Gamble (2014) saw as being major problems for any liberal market economy, but especially the Neoliberal one. He characterised what he calls the 'growth conundrum' as follows:

> *Markets need households and states to reproduce the social and cultural conditions which sustain them. Capital market economies work by privatising gains and socialising losses, but this requires specific institutions to allow this to happen, and there is much room for mismatches and frictions as a result, particularly in distributing the burden of the costs. Under the neo-liberal order an acute form of this conflict has emerged because of the enthusiasm of the neoliberals for giving incentives to the pursuit of private gain by cutting taxes and trying to pay for it by cutting the social costs of reproduction.* (Gamble, 2014: 133)

As well as upsetting the balance between capital and labour, the growth conundrum poses severe problems for democracy:

> *If the total wealth no longer increases, or if the increase is appropriated in the rents that the elites are able to extract as a result of their structural privilege and power, then democratic legitimacy will continue to evaporate and the politics of the extremes will return.* (Gamble, 2014: 154)

The growth conundrum also contributes to the 'fiscal conundrum':

This arises from the tensions between markets and democracies. Achieving legitimation of the market is hard because the way competitive markets work often undermines social cohesion and solidarity. It leads to problems of securing consent for a fiscal base that is strong enough to meet the demands of the people for security and redistribution and to reproduce conditions necessary for successful private accumulation, yet at the same time maintaining external competitiveness and openness. It creates political agendas around issues such as the gap between rich and poor, inequality, universal welfare, immigration, living standards and job protection. (Gamble, 2014: 43)

Finally, there is the 'governance conundrum': the tension between global markets and players (including multinational corporations, the financial markets and intergovernmental organisations) and sovereign states.

These three conundrums can be seen in each of the major crises of Western liberal economies in the past 80 years: the 1930s (beginning with the 1929 stock market crash but with the collapse of the Gold Standard as the key event); the 1970s (triggered by the floating of the dollar in 1971 as the US Government sought to avoid choosing between raising taxes substantially or radically cutting its domestic and overseas spending, reflecting its declining economic competitiveness—cf., Krippner and others); and the 2010 crisis (triggered by the reckless behaviour of the banks but also regulatory errors such as the Fed's decision to put up interest rates in 2005 and the US Government's push to extend home ownership to more low-income families).

As regards the 1970s,

Inflation was brought under control, but over time the mix of neo-liberal policies created a strong deflationary bias in the economy, highly inegalitarian distributive outcomes and a resulting threat of stagnation, both of output and living standards, which undermined the legitimacy of the neo-liberal order. This has driven governments operating within the constraints of the neo-liberal order to pursue privatised Keynesianism rather than welfare Keynesianism, encouraging consumer debt, asset bubbles, financial experimentation and often public deficits in order to boost spending and incomes and correct the deflationary bias. Trying to escape the deflationary trap leads to financial crashes and the prescription of austerity and retrenchment. However, if economies are not to be stuck in deflation and austerity for ever, sooner or later the policies that led to the crash will be tried again. Neo-liberal political economies turn out to be as unstable as Keynesian political economies. (Gamble, 2014: 47)

We have now had slow growth, high debt (both public and private), stagnant living standards and a continuing threat of deflation: Summers's (2013) 'secular stagnation'.

Like Crouch, Blyth, Streeck, and Hacker and Pierson (see Chap. 5), Gamble drew attention to the powerful influence of business:

The privileged position of business which Charles Lindblom analysed in the 1970s, which resulted both from its ability to shape the political agenda through the deployment of its superior resources and from its structural power as the source of employment and growth, has become significantly more privileged in the neo-liberal order. There are major civil society pressure groups which harass business, but it no longer has to contend with a major organised opposing interest (Crouch, 2011). (Gamble, 2014: 13–14)

David Harvey (2005, 2011) offered a broadly similar analysis but put it into the context of the crises of capitalism.

The essence of capitalism is its incessant and relentless drive to capital accumulation (to which all social and political arrangements must yield). This requires the free flow of capital, to which there are many potential limits and barriers.

Money capital scarcities, labour problems, disproportionalities between sectors, natural limits, unbalanced technological and organisational changes (including competition versus monopoly), indiscipline in the labour process and lack of effective demand head up the list. Any one of these circumstances can slow up or disrupt the continuity of capital flow and so produce a crisis that results in the devaluation or loss of capital. When one limit is overcome accumulation often hits up against another somewhere else.

For instance, moves made to alleviate a crisis of labour supply and to curb the political power of organised labour in the 1970s diminished the effective demand for the product, which created difficulties for realisation of the surplus in the market in the 1990s. Moves to alleviate this last problem by extensions of the credit system among the working classes ultimately led to working-class over-indebtedness relative to income that in turn led to a crisis of confidence in the quality of debt instruments (as began to happen in 2006). The crisis tendencies are not resolved but merely moved around. (Harvey, 2011: 117)[7]

In the late 1960s/early 1970s the dollar was under pressure because of the extent of US borrowing. Then the whole system fell into recession, led by the bursting of the global property market bubble in 1973 (before the oil price rise). The New York City fiscal crisis of 1975 (the City was technically bankrupt) centred the storm:

The local solution, orchestrated by an uneasy alliance between state powers and financial institutions, pioneered the neoliberal ideological and practical political turn that was to be deployed worldwide in the struggle to perpetuate and consolidate capitalist class power. The recipe devised was simple enough: crush the power of labour, initiate wage repression, let the market do its work, all the while putting the power of the state at the service of capital in general and investment finance in particular. This was the solution of the 1970s that lies at the root of the crisis of 2008–09. (Harvey, 2011: 172)

The management of the New York fiscal crisis pioneered the way for neoliberal practices both domestically under Reagan and internationally through the IMF in the 1980s. It established the principle that in the event of a conflict between the integrity of financial institutions and bondholders' returns, on the one hand, and the well-being of the citizens on the other, the former was to be privileged. It emphasised the role of government was to create a good business climate rather than look to the needs of the population at large. (Harvey, 2005: 48)[8]

The New York City crisis in turn stemmed from the effort that had been made since the mid-1940s, with heavy borrowing and speculation, to create and sustain 'suburbanisation' and its associated lifestyle ('drive to stay alive and shop until you drop', 'I shop, therefore I am'), which in turn was needed to absorb the postwar surpluses of capital and labour (another central problem for capitalism is how to absorb the surpluses that result from capital accumulation).

Another important cause of the Neoliberal Turn was the desire of capitalists to rid themselves of the cost of the welfare state:

Capital has always had trouble internalising the costs of social reproduction (the care of the young, the ill, the maimed and the aged, the costs of social security, education, and health care). During the 1950s and 1960s many of these social costs were internalised either directly (corporate health care plans and pensions) or indirectly (tax-financed services to the population at large). But the whole period of neoliberal capitalism after the mid-1970s has been marked by a struggle by capital to rid itself of such burdens, leaving it to populations to find their own ways to procure and pay for these services. How we reproduce ourselves is, we have been told by powerful right-wing voices in politics and the media, a matter of personal responsibility, not state obligation. (Harvey, 2011: 265)

The austerity policies adopted in many Western countries since the 2008–09 crisis represent a further step towards the personalisation of the costs of social reproduction.[9]

Another theorist of the crisis of capitalism is Nancy Fraser (2015). Fraser echoes those who see an inherent instability in capitalism:

On the one hand, legitimate, efficacious public power is a condition of possibility for sustained capital accumulation; on the other hand, capitalism's relentless drive to endless capital accumulation tends to destabilise the very public power on which it relies. (Fraser, 2015: 159)

This tendency to self-destabilisation is reinforced by the fact that capitalists almost always place short-term advantage over long-term development.

Following Habermas (1975), Fraser sees capitalist crises as having two phases:

- An administrative phase where public powers lack the necessary heft to govern effectively, possibly because they have been outgunned by private powers (e.g., multinational corporations).
- A legitimation phase where public opinion turns against this failure and seeks to reform the public agencies that can serve the public interest.

The determining factor in whether a full crisis develops is whether a counter-hegemonic discourse emerges to seriously challenge the prevailing 'common sense'. Thus, the replacement of 'managed capitalism' by 'financialised capitalism' was due partly to the failure of the politicians to manage the social and economic upheavals of the late-1960s/early 1970s (an administrative crisis) but also to a legitimation crisis as the New Left criticised the assumptions on which the regime rested. This provided an opportunity for capitalism to be transformed through a combination of old liberal and New Left tropes:

The New Left mounted a counter-hegemonic challenge to the reigning assump-
tions about subjective agency, public power, society, justice and history in state
managed capitalism. This challenge proved sufficiently powerful to de-
legitimate that regime but not powerful enough to dictate the basic direction of
its transformation. On the contrary, New Left assumptions were themselves
hegemonized, recuperated into an emergent new common sense, which now per-
vades financialized capitalism. (Fraser, 2015: 181)

The bridge was the entrepreneurial mode of subjectification identified
by Wendy Brown and others described in Chap. 2.

Fraser observes that many of the conditions for an administrative crisis
of financialised capitalism were already in place following the 2008 crash.
But even if there were a credible counter-hegemonic challenge, public
power was now so weakened and contested that whereas previously the
problem was marshalling sufficient (and sufficiently passivised) legitimation for the expanded use of state capacity to secure the conditions for
ongoing accumulation and private appropriation of the social surplus, the
problem now is with the state power itself. The basic dilemma is: how can
democratic forces fix a dysfunctional system when the instrument needed
for the repair is itself being ground to dust by those very same system
dynamics? This is the crisis of the crisis of capitalism.

4.10   The Decline of the Left

Richard Rorty (1998) also criticised the American Left for giving the
Right the opportunity to exploit the impact of globalisation and downsizing on the labour market and many American households. The 'reformist
Left', inspired by Dewey and Whitman, had believed that the US was
flawed yet perfectible. But shame over the treatment of African Americans
and other minorities within the country, and the waging of the Vietnam
War externally, led the Left to give up trying to change the country's institutions and instead focus on its victims: 'naming the system' took prece-
dence over reforming the laws. Cultural and identity politics replaced the
politics of social and economic justice:

[The] *cultural Left thinks more about stigma than about money, more about*
deep and hidden psychosexual motivations than about shallow and evident
greed. (Rorty, 1998: 77)[10]

The Left's consequent failure to tackle 'socially accepted sadism' (the treatment of blacks and other minorities), at the same time as economic inequality and insecurity were rising, left it wide open to challenge from the Right:

> It has been left to scurrilous demagogues like Patrick [sic] Buchanan to take political advantage of the widening gap between rich and poor. While the Left's back was turned, the bourgeoisification of the white proletariat which began in World War II and continued up through the Vietnam War has been halted, and the process has gone into reverse. America is now proletarianizing its bourgeoisie, and this process is likely to culminate in a bottom-up populist revolt, of the sort Buchanan hopes to foment. (Rorty, 1998: 83)

> Members of labor unions, and unorganized unskilled workers, will sooner or later realize that their government is not even trying to prevent wages from sinking or to prevent jobs from being exported. Around the same time, they will realize that suburban white-collar workers – themselves desperately afraid of being downsized – are not going to let themselves be taxed to provide social benefits for someone else.
>
> At that point, something will crack. The nonsuburban electorate will decide that the system has failed and start looking for a strongman to vote for – someone who will assure them that, once he is elected, the smug bureaucrats, tricky lawyers, overpaid bond salesmen, and postmodernist professors will no longer be calling the shots ...
>
> One thing that is very likely to happen is that the gains made in the past forty years by black and brown Americans, and by homosexuals, will be wiped out. Jocular contempt for women will come back into fashion. The words "nigger" and "kike" will once again be heard in the workplace. All the sadism that the academic Left tried to make unacceptable to its students will come flooding back. All the resentments which badly educated Americans feel about having their manners dictated to them by college graduates will find an outlet. (Rorty, 1998: 89–90)

In the Trump era, this all seems remarkably prescient (for a similar, and earlier, critique in Britain, see Hall, S. 1979).

4.11   CONCLUSION

In this chapter we reviewed a number of theories that attempt to explain the Neoliberal Turn in structural terms, particularly developments in market capitalism. In the next chapter we look at theories that, by contrast, emphasise the activities of institutions and individuals in particular political economies.

Notes

1. We noted in Chap. 3 the increased concentration of economic power associated with deregulation. A number of writers have written about the paradox that whatever the theory, in practice Neoliberalism needs a strong state: William Davies (2014: 25) quotes Jamie Peck (2008: 39) 'Neoliberalism's curse has been that it can live neither with, nor without, the state' (see Chap. 7).
2. Polanyi (1944) provided the earliest and still one of the best critiques of Neoliberalism. His essential point was that if you attempt to embed society in the economy—rather than see the economy as embedded in society—you will end up with serious social disruption that in turn can undermine democracy, the rise of Fascism in the 1930s in Europe being a case in point. We shall return to these issues in Chaps. 6 and 7.
3. Crouch (2009) adds the growth of derivatives and futures markets among the wealthy in the 1990s and 2000s.
4. For the 'efficient market hypothesis', see Malkiel, 2003.
5. Kevin P. Gallagher and Richard Kozul-Wright (2022) argue for a new Bretton Woods to make good the reforms to promote stability, social inclusion and sustainability that were promised after the 2008–09 crisis, but never delivered. This was echoed by the US Treasury Secretary, Janet Yellen, at the Atlantic Council in April 2022 (Fouriezos 2022).
6. Streeck also (2017: xxxv, note 37) draws attention to the linkages between loose monetary policy, household debt, housing market bubbles and the likelihood of financial crises.
7. By 'disproportionalities between sectors' is meant the fact that such things as the uneven development of technological capacities across sectors produce imbalances in the output of wage goods versus means of production (Harvey, 2011: 95).
8. In her 2009 book, Kim Phillips-Fein describes how the young Donald Trump exploited the crisis to gain tax breaks worth $360 m (as of 2016) in return for a one-off investment of $9.5 m.
9. Writers advancing a similar explanation include Edsall (1985), George (2000) and Dumenil & Levy (2004a and 2004b).
10. For a more recent statement of this position, see Lilla (2016).

References

Bell, D. (1978). *The cultural contradictions of Capitalism*. Basic Books.
Blyth, M. (2002). *Great transformations: Economic ideas and institutional change in the twentieth century*. Cambridge University Press.
Clarke, S. (1988). *Keynesianism, Monetarism and the crisis of the state*. Edward Elgar.

Crouch, C. (2009). Privatised Keynesianism: An unacknowledged policy regime. *The British Journal of Politics and International Relations, 11*, 382–399.

Crouch, C. (2011). *The strange non-death of Neoliberalism*. Polity Press.

Davies, W. (2014). *The limits of Neoliberalism: Authority, sovereignty and the logic of competition*. Sage.

Davis, G. F. (2009). *Managed by the markets: How finance reshaped America*. Oxford University Press.

Dumenil, G., & Levy, D. (2004a). *Capital resurgent: Roots of the Neoliberal revolution*. Harvard University Press.

Dumenil, G., & Levy, D. (2004b). Neoliberal income trends: Wealth, class and ownership in the USA. *New Left Review, 30*, 105–133.

Edsall, T. (1985). *The new politics of inequality*. Norton.

Foroohar, R. (2016). *Makers and takers: The rise of finance and the fall of American business*. Crown Business.

Fouriezos, N. (2022, April 13). *Janet Yellen's message to the world: There can be no 'sitting on the fence' on Russia*. Retrieved June 21, 2022, from https://www.atlanticcouncil.org/blogs/new-atlanticist/janet-yellens-message-to-the-world-there=can-be-no-sitting-on-the-fence-on-russia.

Fraser, N. (2015, Fall). Legitimation crisis? On the political contradictions of financialized Capitalism. *Critical Historical Studies, 2*(2), 157–189.

Gallagher, K. P., & Kozul-Wright, R. (2022). *The case for a new Bretton woods*. Polity.

Gamble, A. (2014). *Crisis without end? The unravelling of Western prosperity*. Palgrave Macmillan.

George, S. (2000). A short history of Neoliberalism: Twenty years of elite economics and emerging opportunities for structural change. In W. Bello, N. Bullard, & K. Malhotra (Eds.), *Global finance: New thinking on regulating capital markets* (pp. 27–35). Zed Books.

Habermas, J. (1975). *Legitimation crisis* (T. McCarthy, Trans.). Beacon.

Hall, S. (1979, January, 14–20). The great moving right show. *Marxism Today*.

Harvey, D. (2005). *A brief history of Neoliberalism*. Oxford University Press.

Harvey, D. (2011). *The enigma of capital and the crises of Capitalism*. Profile.

Helleiner, E. (1994). *States and the reemergence of global finance: From Bretton Woods to the 1990s*. Cornell University Press.

Klein, N. (2017). *No is not enough: Defeating the new shock politics*. Allen Lane.

Krippner, G. R. (2011). *Capitalizing on crisis: The political origins of the rise of finance*. Harvard University Press.

Lansley, S. (2011). *The cost of inequality: Three decades of the super-rich and the economy*. Gibson Square.

Lilla, M. (2016, November 18). The end of identity liberalism. *The New York Times*.

Malkiel, B. G. (2003). The efficient market hypothesis and its Critics. *Journal of Economic Perspectives, 17*(1), 59–82.

Peck, J. (2008). Remaking laissez-faire. *Progress in Human Geography, 32*(1), 3–43.

Pettifor, A. (2006). *The coming first world debt crisis.* Palgrave Macmillan.

Phillips-Fein, K. (2009). *Invisible hands: The making of the conservative movement from the New Deal to Reagan.* W. W. Norton.

Polanyi, K. (1944). *The great transformation: The political and economic origins of our time.* Beacon Press.

Reich, R. (2016). *Saving capitalism: For the many, not the few.* Icon Books.

Rorty, R. (1998). *Achieving our country: Leftist thought in twentieth-century America.* Harvard University Press.

Rose, R., & Peters, G. (1978). *Can government go bankrupt?* Basic Books.

Ruggie, J. (1982). International regimes, transactions, and change: Embedded Liberalism in the postwar economic order. *International Organization, 36,* 379–415.

Stein, J. (2010). *Pivotal decade: How the United States traded factories for finance in the seventies.* Yale University Press.

Streeck, W. (2017). *Buying time: The delayed crisis of democratic Capitalism* (2nd ed.). Verso.

Summers, L. (2013, November 8). *Transcript of Larry summers speech at the IMF economic forum.* Retrieved November 19, 2014, from http://www.facebook.com/notes/randy-fellmy/transcript-of-larry-summers-speech-at-the-imf-economic-forum-nov-8-2013/585630634864563.

Tomaskovic-Devey, D., & Lin, K.-H. (2011). Income dynamics, economic rents, and the financialization of the U.S. economy. *American Sociological Review, 76*(4), 538–559.

CHAPTER 5

Explaining the Neoliberal Turn Institutional Theories

Abstract In Chap. 4 we looked at structural explanations for the Neoliberal Turn. In this chapter we discuss theories that emphasise the roles of institutions, actors and cultures. We use the following headings: the politics of decline, the rise and fall of democratic globalism, pivotal decade, winner-take-all politics, pathways of development, a superpower transformed, the rise of the right and false consciousness.

Keywords President Nixon • President Reagan • Prime Minister Thatcher

5.1   THE POLITICS OF DECLINE

In *Reagan, Thatcher and the Politics of Decline* Joel Krieger (1986) argued that both Reagan and Thatcher took advantage of the fact that existing centrist politicians (Heath and Callaghan in the UK, the liberal Republicans in the US) were tarnished by their failure to cope with the 1970s economic crisis. The new leaders might have tried to tackle the longer-term structural problems of economic performance and declining geopolitical influence that had made dealing with the crisis harder. Instead, both appealed to a clever mix of patriotism, family values and resentment (in both countries, against the unions; in the US, against blacks and other

R. Brown, *The Conservative Counter-Revolution in Britain and America 1980–2020*,
https://doi.org/10.1007/978-3-031-09142-1_5

minorities; in the UK, against immigrants). Both also focused on the sub-urban vote.

This was a conscious attempt to reverse the 'integrationist' tendencies of 'welfare Keynesianism'. But for this to succeed, scapegoats were needed:

> *Whatever their ostensible purpose and design, the economic policies of Reagan, like those of Thatcher, are best understood politically as displacement strategies. But whilst Thatcher must deflect failure inwards* [for instance, onto miners goaded into a strike by a Government-led colliery closure programme] *greater economic and geopolitical influence still permits the US to enjoy the considerable privilege of socialising the costs of its economic decline globally, pushing the consequences of economic mismanagement outward.* (Krieger, 1986: 167)[1]

The Reagan/Thatcher counter-revolution also required a willingness to use the full powers of the state, made somewhat easier by the fact that both leaders were 'outsiders' better able to insulate themselves from the customary pressures from economic and political elites:

> *Economic mismanagement (external deficits, failures of growth) does not derail the Reagan and Thatcher governments because their insularity from traditional pressures renders economic problems more amenable to political manipulation than is usually the case. No policy can lose, so long as they can make the victims pay for the Government's mistakes.* (Krieger, 1986: 169)[2]

This statement could also apply to recent British Governments' austerity policies (Wren-Lewis, 2018).

But there was no Thatcher 'economic miracle':

> *It is often taken for granted in media and policy making circles that more structural economic reforms, involving greater labour market flexibility, will increase the efficiency of the economy. We make no such assumption. Instead the purpose of this report is to assess the factual evidence on the macro-economic impact of liberal policies on the UK economy. In particular it is to assess their impact on the growth of GDP, productivity, employment, unemployment and inflation. The report shows that GDP and productivity have grown more slowly since 1979 than over previous decades, contrary to widespread belief. Although inflation and industrial disruption were reduced after 1980, unemployment and inequality have been higher. The volatility of the economic growth has also been much greater.* (Coutts & Gudgin, 2015: 5, original authors' emphasis; for similar findings, see Henry, 2014, and Wren-Lewis 2015)

Beatty and Fothergill (2016) argued that the main effect of the job losses of the 1980s was to divert large numbers of men and women in the old industrial areas onto capacity-related benefits. These people were now bearing the brunt of the austerity-related welfare cuts that were intended to bring the social security budget down. So it could not be a coincidence that these areas voted 2 to 1 for Brexit. Another report from the same centre (Beatty et al., 2017) suggests that the real level of unemployment is much higher than official estimates and that only much of southern and eastern England outside London, with real unemployment in the 2–3% range, can really be said to be operating at full employment (for a similar conclusion, see Bell & Blanchflower, 2018).[3]

As regards the US, Robert Gordon, in a 2018 review of a recent history of American capitalism (Greenspan & Wooldridge, 2018), wrote:

> *The book ends with an America in decline. Greenspan and Wooldridge recognise that "more Americans are living better lives than ever before" and paint a stunning portrait of the multidimensional improvement in living conditions since the late 19th century. Otherwise the omens are bleak. Productivity growth since 2010 has slowed to a trickle, creative destruction is drying up, labour mobility is ossifying, and business concentration is rising as firms protect themselves with "all sorts of walls and moats". Beside overregulation, the underlying evil is the growth of corporate entitlements, which crowd out investment spending which in turn pinches productivity growth.*

It may also be worth observing that—at least in the opinion of some experts—there was a feasible alternative to the Reagan/Thatcher approach. In a scholarly review of the various explanations for the failure to control the US inflation that began around 1965, Thomas Mayer (1999) concluded that whilst cognitive errors, political pressures and a wish to avoid interest rate fluctuations had all played their part, the biggest single factor was the intellectual atmosphere. The Keynesian economists at the Fed were much more concerned with unemployment. This meant that when the monetary correction came it was too little, too late (cf. the quotation at the head of Chap. 4).

5.2   The Rise and Fall of Democratic Globalism

Robert Kuttner (2018) looks at how the Bretton Woods regime of regulated internationalism that we discussed in Chap. 4 supported a mixed economy in both Europe and the US, and how it was undone by several convergent events between the late 1950s and the early 1970s. These included the collapse of fixed exchange rates and capital controls (which invited a return to financial speculation); the increased inflation that followed the breakdown of Bretton Woods and the oil price rises (which undercut consensual wage bargaining); and the 'tight money' response of conservative finance ministers and central bankers (which led to the combination of high unemployment and inflation).

All of these shifts tilted the balance between labour and capital decisively back to capital, especially finance. By the late-1970s, these economic reversals and policy challenges had discredited the governing parties that were then mostly centrist. The inflation crisis of the 1970s was a political windfall for resurgent conservatism. Yet,

> *this shift back to radical* laissez-faire *– neoliberalism – was not required by the economic circumstances. Neither was the full deregulation of finance, nor the enforcement of austerity, nor the use of trade rules to further undermine domestic managed capitalism, nor the indulgence of globalized and systematic tax evasion. These turned out to be economic failures, except in the one sense that they shifted incomes to the top.* (Kuttner, 2018: 73)

5.3   Pivotal Decade

In *Pivotal Decade: How the United States Traded Factories for Finance in the Seventies*, Judith Stein (2010) argued that it was the events and decisions of the 1970s, and particularly 1976–80, that took the US from the Age of Compression (Goldin & Margo, 1991) to the Age of Inequality, from the fear of unemployment to the fear of inflation.

The rises in the prices of oil and food and the associated general inflation in the early and late-1970s posed challenges that the conventional Keynesian polices of managing aggregate demand to ensure economic stability could not overcome. But political factors also played their part, with Jimmy Carter regarded as a weak President who saw the main domestic challenges as cultural and social rather than economic—in part, a legacy of the Democrats' shift to 'identity politics' in the late-1960s/early

1970s—up against an attractive Republican candidate whose tax-cutting messages had a certain resonance with voters whose taxes had increased with inflation.

But there were also some longer-running causes:

- Longstanding weaknesses in productivity on the part of domestic producers, partially disguised by America's postwar political and economic dominance.
- A continuing belief in free trade, both for its own sake and because it was felt necessary to protect the US-led anti-Communist order.
- The increasing threat to US producers posed by overseas suppliers through globalisation, but which also facilitated offshoring and downsizing.
- Financialisation and the increasing role played in both the economy and politics by Wall Street. This reinforced the tendency of the Federal Government to put the needs of the international economy ahead of the domestic one.
- The decline of the labour unions alongside a more assertive business community.
- Greater fluidity in politics as internal reforms reduced the power of party bosses and made them more open to outsider 'capture'.

There are some obvious parallels with Britain.

The outcomes were greater inequality, continuing and chronic internal and external deficits, lower investment and productivity, greater poverty and debt, greater economic instability, and higher unemployment. There was also a shift in the composition of the economy, towards non-tradeable sectors like real estate, financial services and defence:

Between 1973 and 1990, GDP grew 1.06, compared with 2.45 from 1950 to 1973. The rapid gains after the 1982 recession did not continue and savings, investment and productivity stagnated. Deregulation spawned the savings and loan crisis, not entrepreneurship. (Stein, 2010: 275)

Again, there are clear parallels with the UK.

Stein noted that Neoliberal policies were not the preserve only of Republicans. It was the Democrats under Carter (pushed by Ralph Nader's consumerism) who started deregulation and abolished credit controls. It was the 1978 Congressional Democrats' tax cuts that stimulated the property tax revolt that Jack Kemp and then Reagan latched onto. Clinton's tax cuts were the biggest after 1981. Clinton also began the deregulation of Wall Street with the Finance Services Modernisation and Commodity Futures Modernisation acts. Republican leaders up to and including Nixon accepted the New Deal (President Eisenhower's 'modern Republicanism'). It was only with Barry Goldwater and then President Ford that the Republicans began on the rightward path that has continued to this day.

5.4   Winner-Take-All Politics

Jacob Hacker and Paul Pierson are amongst those who have argued for an institutional explanation for the Neoliberal Turn and what followed it.

The starting point of *Winner-Take-All-Politics* (2010) was the enormous growth in economic inequality between the late-1970s and the mid-2000s. This was not just about the wealthy having a disproportionate share of the proceeds of growth:

> *It is also how they have managed to restructure the economy to shift the risks of their new economic playground downward, saddling Americans with greater debt, tearing new holes in the safety net, and imposing broad financial risks on Americans as workers, investors, taxpayers.* (13).

There has been a tilting of the American political landscape:

> *Ascendant business groups have gained ground, as has a mobilised evangelical movement that brings less affluent voters into unexpected alliance with these powerful economic interests through the GOP. At the same time, the broad set of organizations that once brought ordinary voters into politics* [e.g., the unions] *giving them knowledge and leverage and might, have lost ground.* (160)

Business had upped its political game in the 1970s as a response to the liberal policies of both Democrat and Republican administrations. The two main political parties had adjusted to this shift in power, but

> *the source of the problem is the huge and real economic schism that separates the overwhelming majority of Americans … from the tiny slice that has reaped the lion's share of economic growth.*
> *From 1979 until 2006, the top 1 percent received 36 percent of all the income growth generated in the American economy, while the highest-income 1/10th of*

*1 percent – one out of every 1000 households – received nearly 20 percent, even after taking into account all federal taxes and all government and employer-provided benefits … To explain **this** split – how the United States morphed from the Broadland of shared prosperity that defined the immediate decades after World War II into our present Richistan of hyperconcentrated rewards at the top – technological change and globalization prove to be of surprisingly limited relevance. They matter, to be sure. But what matters more is how these forces have been chaneled by major changes in what government has done and not done over the course of the thirty-year war. Where the conventional wisdom confidently declares, "It's the economy", we find, again and again, "It's the politics".* (Hacker & Pierson, 2010: 290, original authors' emphasis; see also Drutman, 2015; Katz, 2015; Lafer, 2017)

In *American Amnesia* (2016) Hacker and Pierson updated this thesis, but their main argument was that the historically successful American partnership between the state and the market was now at risk from a combination of diverging economic interests and the organised groups that were exacerbating these divergences and for whom denigrating and denying the state were cardinal. They identified

an enormous shift in power towards a new corporate elite much more hostile to the mixed economy, much less constrained by moderates in government or by organised labor, and much more in tune with the new celebration of the 'free market' (p. 172).[4]

Let Them Eat Tweets (2020) describes the US as a 'plutocracy': 'government of, by and for the rich, irrespective of the broader interests of American society' (p. 1). This involves the following:

- tax cuts for corporations and the very rich;
- welfare cuts to pay for them;
- rolling back environmental, consumer, labour and financial protections;
- attempts to strip health insurance from millions of Americans;
- conservatising the courts through appointments to the Federal judiciary;

even though none of these has popular support (even amongst Republican voters).

The key development here was the Grand Old Party's (G.O.P) embrace of plutocracy:

Starting as a standard-issue centre-right party, the GOP has mutated into an ultra-conservative insurgent force, and one that casts its lot with plutocracy even as plutocracy's rise endangered the economic security and opportunities of many of its voters (p.41).

This statement could also apply to the British Conservatives since 1979. Hacker and Pierson coined the term 'plutocratic populism': 'a bitter brew of reactionary economic priorities and right wing cultural and racial appeals' (p.5). Accordingly, Trump is not an anti-establishment insurgent, but a consequence and enabler of the Party's long march to the right. He campaigned on an anti-plutocratic agenda, but

the plutocrats have gotten huge tax cuts. They have reaped the benefits of an unprecedented attack on regulations that police big corporations and protect consumers, workers, and the environment. And they have seen the nation's powerful courts tilt even further in favor of elite economic interests. (p. 142)

Hacker and Pierson emphasise the role of the courts in promoting the plutocratic agenda:

When they are not weighing in on the culture wars, the courts offer ample opportunity for plutocrats to achieve victories they could not win more directly at the polls: scaling back regulations, curtailing the opportunities for class-action lawsuits, which help level the playing field for disputes between powerful corporations and workers or consumers; and blocking or offering corporate-friendly interpretations of federal laws. Just as important, conservative courts can shift the rules of political life in favor of their allies: easing the flow of dark money, protecting gerrymandering, allowing efforts to disenfranchise voters. Judicial restrictions on unions, which have proliferated in recent years, are particularly attractive, because they strengthen corporations in the private economy and weaken a key ally of the Democratic Party (recall how much union membership has mattered in recent elections). (p. 161)

They also highlight the advantages that the unreformed US Constitution gives the G.O.P:

Our system's emphasis on representing particular geographic areas, the tilt of the Senate toward low-population states, and the separation of powers – the fragmentation of political authority among Congress, the president, the courts and state governments. (p. 205)

5.5   Pathways of Development

In Chap. 3 we noted that Monica Prasad's 'adversarial political economy' was one of the reasons for associating increased inequality in the US and UK with Neoliberal policies. Prasad (2006) identified the key features of Neoliberalism as being tax structures that favour capital accumulation over redistribution, industrial policies that minimise the state's role in relation to private entities and retrenchment in welfare spending. She looked at how each of these issues was handled in the US, UK, Germany and France between the mid-1970s and the early 2000s. She rejected most of the other theories for the rise of Neoliberalism: globalisation and capital flight, class-based explanations (business and labour), Neoliberal ideas or differences in national cultures.

Instead, she introduced two sets of ideas: the importance of state institutions as 'actors' in the policy process (and not simply as conduits for other pressures) and 'path dependency', whereby patterns established at moments of crisis can influence events long afterwards. This led her to identify two different types of political economy: as nation building (Germany and France) or as justice (the US and UK).

In Germany and France the postwar emphasis was on rebuilding through economic growth. Political decision making was subordinated to corporate decision making (Germany) or academic experts (France). These institutions enabled the two countries' governments to resist and transform the new social pressures arising from the oil crisis (it is also relevant that the Left was out of power for much of the postwar period in both countries). But in the US and UK, where governments alternated between Right and Left, 'adversarial' politics developed. Decisions on tax, industrial policy and welfare often reflected the view that the goal of the political economy was justice: redistributing from rich to poor, protecting workers and consumers, lifting people out of poverty. She summarised her argument thus:

> *Free market, or neoliberal, policies did not result from any pragmatic or rational analysis showing that they were the best way to manage the crisis; nor were they the result of globalization, business-group pressure, or national culture. Rather, they arose where the political-economic structure was adversarial. States in which the political-economic structure defined labor and capital as adversaries and the middle class and the poor in opposition to one another (the middle class paying for policies that benefit the poor) provided the potential to ally the majority of voters with market-friendly policies, and certain structural*

changes provided incentives to politicians to mobilize this potential. (Prasad, 2006: 38)[5]

By 'structural changes' Prasad means changes that weakened the power of Congressional committees and seniority in Congress which were the outcome of social pressures in the 1960s and 1970s to give 'power to the people'. These changes incidentally made the political parties more vulnerable to outsider 'capture' (as already noted).

Prasad draws attention to one of the problems when capitalism and democracy meet: how to protect the interests of the poor when the majority is not poor and it is the majority that rules:

> *When the majority of citizens become taxpayers and move out of the working class, especially under certain economic and decision-making structures, support for redistribution to the poor (as opposed to redistribution from the rich) is fragile. If politics is particularly competitive, politicians will take advantage of this fragility in their quest for power. This is the story of neoliberalism in the United States and, in a different way, in Britain. The comparison with France and Germany shows that the divergent outcomes arose not because of cultural differences but because the nonadversarial political-economic structure in France and Germany meant that there was less room for an electoral appeal to neoliberalism.* (Prasad, 2006: 39–40)

In short,

> *different decision-making structures and policies mobilized the electorate in different ways in the two sets of countries, so that in West Germany and France, pro-growth policies and state structures meant that politicians were neither forced to make neoliberal appeals to the electorate to stay in power, nor able to find issues that would appeal to a broad segment of the electorate. In the United States and Britain, in the wake of the 1973 oil crisis, the adversarial structure of previous policies led to the potential popularity of neoliberalism, and adversarial state structures led to a greater need for politicians to mobilize populist appeals to acquire or maintain power.* (Prasad, 2006: 41–42)

Like Joel Krieger, Prasad stresses the contingent, incremental and only partially coherent nature of the policies pursued by Reagan and Thatcher. Reagan picked up on the tax cuts already being popularised by others (Proposition 13 in California, Jack Kemp) and cut funding for environmental regulation. But he shied away from other liberalising measures because of consumer resistance, as well as from radical welfare reforms that would have upset the middle classes. Thatcher soon abandoned Monetarism, only embarked on privatisation as a means of obtaining the revenues needed to modernise British Telecom, was as surprised as her advisers when it proved popular, and (unlike some of her successors) refrained from attacking the middle-class welfare state (the NHS, education, universal benefits like Child Benefit). Nevertheless, the Reagan tax cuts and Thatcher's sale of Council houses, as well as the deliberate weakening of the unions, changed both societies permanently.

In a further book, Prasad (2011) argued that the real difference between the US and most major European countries lay in state attitudes towards consumption:

> *While European countries focused on top-down efforts at reconstructing their economies by focusing on production and restraining consumption, the United States pioneered a form of "mortgage Keynesianism" in which mortgage finance was a primary mechanism for sustaining economic growth. These developments in turn yielded a political economy that undermined the public welfare state and established dependence on the development of credit-financed private consumption for economic growth, in contrast to the production-oriented economies of Europe* [where welfare states were either an explicit pro quo for wage restraint or were a piecemeal response to the instabilities being caused by that economic growth]. (Prasad, 2011: 93; cf. Crouch's 'privatised Keynesianism')

Prasad comments:

> *While a political economy based on credit may offer a measure of relief to those who are able to borrow, it leaves unprotected those who are not. In undermining the welfare state, the American path of democratization of credit condemns a segment of the populace to poverty. Moreover ... a more developed welfare state in the US would have constrained the growth of credit and thus the growth of American consumption. As the world economy has depended for many years on the foundation of strong consumption in the US, it may not be unwarranted to conclude that the prosperity of the world in recent decades has been built on the consignment of a segment of the American population to poverty.* (Prasad, 2011: 244–245)[6]

In her most recent (2018) book, Prasad attempts to show why and how tax cuts—and especially tax cuts for individuals—became and remained a key feature of US political life from the 1960s onwards. She attributes this process—begun by Kennedy-Johnson in 1964—to four factors:

- the slowdown in growth in the 1960s combined with the rise in inflation in the 1970s;
- America's greater exposure to inflation because (a) its political economy was geared to consumption and maintaining purchasing power, as the world's 'consumer of last resort', with home owner-ship substituting for the welfare state, and (b) America's tax struc-ture was dominated by direct taxes that were more vulnerable to inflation, hence the greater need for a policy against inflation;
- the Republicans' need—especially in the wake of Watergate and Gerald Ford's defeat in the 1976 presidential election—for a dis-tinctive but broadly popular policy. Here she notes the initiative seized by Jack Kemp (although, ironically, he started with business taxes) and Reagan, with an unerring ability to 'see where the votes were', even though tax cuts were not seen by most people as a major issue as compared with inflation (political demagoguery again). 'Tax cut clientelism' replaced 'welfare state clientelism'.[7] Again, there are some clear parallels with Mrs. Thatcher;
- financialisation and globalisation—the internationalisation of cap-ital—meant that deficits ceased to be an objection. The markets could live with them and so therefore could the voters.

Prasad denies that the Reagan tax cuts were part of a wider Neoliberal agenda although some of that certainly followed. They were not driven by ideology, economists' ideas, racism or business (although business cer-tainly wanted to be put on the same competitive footing as their interna-tional competitors and has finally got there with the Trump tax cuts—see Note 12 below). It is true that deregulation, the reduction of the unions, Monetarism and free trade accompanied the tax cuts, but many of these were also espoused by the Democrats.

Bracket creep (the way in which inflation automatically takes earners into a higher tax bracket) was already recognised as an issue. The Reagan cuts were reversed (it was the Volcker-inspired recession that dealt with the inflation). It was only with President H.W. Bush that tax cuts became a permanent feature so that it is only quite recently—when economic inequality is at pre-1914 levels—that tax increases are once again begin-ning to be seriously talked about. The Republicans persisted with tax cuts

because they had no alternative policy (see below), the Democrats because they saw them as popular.
Prasad sums up the significance of the Reagan cuts thus:

> *What Reagan's tax cut actually did was enable future tax cuts – by demonstrating the political appeal of cutting taxes even at the expense of deficits and by eventually showing that deficits could be financed with foreign borrowing – and those further tax cuts have had an effect. Thanks to them, the share of American tax revenue has held stable as a percentage of GDP even though in other countries tax revenue as a percentage of GDP tends to rise as GDP rises.*
> (Prasad, 2018: 161)

Elsewhere, she notes that government spending has continued at pretty much the same levels as before. There has been no increase in economic growth or innovation, quite the opposite. But the tax cuts may have stopped the state from being able to respond to new challenges such as the impact of automation on the workplace or climate change.[8]

Prasad's view of Reagan's tax cuts as a contingent piece of political opportunism is echoed in Isaac William Martin's, 2008 study *The Permanent Tax Revolt: How the Property Tax Transformed American Politics*. The revolt against the property tax that began in California in the mid-1960s, and on which Jack Kemp and then Ronald Reagan capitalised, was the outcome (ironically) of the need to bolster public expenditure at a time when economic and social changes were subjecting the limited American welfare state to unprecedented strain.

5.6 A Superpower Transformed

A comprehensive study by Deutsche Bank Markets Research (Reid et al., 2017) identified the August 71 dollar float as the point at which the financial crises that have plagued us over the past half-century began to accumulate (see also, Authers, 2017). In the book with the above title, Daniel J. Sargent (2015) discussed how the US sought to cope with the challenges that the 1970s crisis posed both to its international hegemony and to its domestic political economy.

Sargent described how several informed observers at the time noted that the postwar settlement of the new architecture for collective security (through the UN) and an economic regime enabling international trade to co-exist with welfare states (Bretton Woods)—both according to the central role to the US—was by the late-1960s/early 1970s breaking up through the ossification of the Cold War and the resurgence of globalisation (the value of offshore financial holdings surged from 1.2 per cent of world GDP in 1964 to 16.2 per cent in 1980, world trade tripling over the same period—p. 5):

> *The remaking of the capitalist order that turned on the 1970s was neither the result of a neoliberal counter-revolution nor the achievement of self-conscious design. Rather, globalization produced a disjuncture between territorial politics and transnational economics that empowered markets at the expense of government. For the American superpower, globalization conferred benefits, but it also left democracy diminished, curtailing the capacities of representative institutions. Globalization without governance also left open the question of how global dilemmas, such as climate change and financial crises, might be engaged, much less managed.* (Sargent, 2015: 10)

Sargent analysed the factors behind President Nixon's decision to unhook the dollar from gold. Nixon was aware that declining American competitiveness threatened its political and economic hegemony, with the deterioration in its external account from the mid-1960s, making it harder to finance overseas military commitments or resist domestic calls for protectionism. Sargent quotes from an end of 1971 analysis by the Chair of the Council on International Economic Policy, Peter Peterson:

> *Far from being the "arsenal of democracy", as Franklin Roosevelt had envisaged, the United States was looking increasingly like a rentier superpower, Peterson concluded, "engaged largely in services, drawing income from foreign investments, and importing more goods than it exports."* (Sargent, 2015: 101)

This description applies just as well to the UK today.

The chosen solution—which would improve the trade balance, put Americans back to work and help the President's chances of re-election—was the devaluation of the dollar (which was indeed achieved temporarily). This also averted the domestic retrenchment and curtailment of consumption that would otherwise have been needed (as the German Chancellor, Willy Brandt, pointed out). However, it was not intended—at least not by the President—to lead to the dismantlement of Bretton Woods.

The real problem was the unwillingness of governments collectively to eschew unilateral action of this kind and attempt the international cooperation (and the limitations on national policy autonomy) that would be needed to put the genie of liberalised financial markets back in the bottle:

The postwar order depended on a containment of finance, which the Bretton Woods institutions consecrated. It also depended on the United States: the dollar was the bedrock of postwar international monetary stability, and Washington disbursed economic resources to its Cold War allies and clients, fostering their recovery and growth. In the 1960s this postwar order fractured. Globalization undid the postwar containment of finance, while the decline of US economic power destabilized an international order organized around the dollar. Governments managed in 1971 to devise a new matrix of fixed exchange rates [the Smithsonian agreement to incorporate the effective devaluation of the dollar against some other major currencies] *but they did not reconcile monetary stability to financial globalization. Instead, they accepted floating currencies in 1973, ceding power over exchange rates to foreign exchange markets, and began to abolish capital controls. Still, what ensued after Bretton Woods was not a new international order keyed to neoliberal purposes but a prolonged phase of improvisation and disorder.* (Sargent, 2015: 298)

Sargent notes that Paul Volcker's October 1979 system of monetary targeting subjected the US to the first significant monetary discipline since August 1971:

Volcker did not act eagerly, but he saw few alternatives if inflation were to be curbed and the dollar's global role sustained. The consequences would include the severest recession and worst unemployment since the Great Depression. Governments elsewhere made similar choices. Margaret Thatcher embraced monetary discipline with missionary zeal, while France, in 1983–84, undertook a reluctant tournant to the market under a socialist president. Such choices were dramatic, but the retreat of managed capitalism in the 1970s owed to complex causes, some of which were endogenous to the old order. Managed capitalism faltered in the late 1960s, as productivity growth slowed and inflation mounted. Globalization also proved to be powerfully disruptive. Interdependence loosened the control of governments over their economies, which inhibited the management of national economies and prompted decision-makers, after experimenting with collaborative coordination, to submit instead to the discipline of integrating markets. (Sargent, 2015: 299)

In his 2017 biography of Richard Nixon, John Farrell described how the President came to take the fateful decision to let the dollar float. The decision was in fact part of a package that also included wage and price controls and a 10 per cent tax on imports (from a Republican President). Together with the devalued dollar, the border tax would raise the costs of imports, create jobs at home and reassure the electorate. The package was a response to the stagflation that in turn was largely due to the costs of the Vietnam War and the unwillingness of successive Presidents to cut back on popular programmes to relieve the pressures on the public finances. Other drivers were the fact that US dollars held in foreign banks (the result of increased overseas spending by American consumers, corporations and investors) far outstripped the Government's holding of gold, the President's desire to be seen as revolutionising international economics at the same time as he was revolutionising international diplomacy through the opening to China and, last but not least, his need to be re-elected in November 1972.

As Farrell noted, whilst the President upset his allies, his economic manoeuvring helped him to clinch re-election. Inflation was held at 3 per cent and unemployment actually fell to 5.5 per cent by Election Day. But once the controls were lifted, inflation resumed its upward march, reinforced by the Arabs. The consequential increases in inflation and unemployment and the drop in GDP and share prices corroded the President's support in the run-up to Watergate.

According to Farrell's account (which benefitted from recently published archives) the decision to let the dollar float was not part of any deeper or longer-term plan for either the US or the international economy, whether Neoliberal or of any other kind:

> *They were improvising, making it up as they went along, eking it out to November 1972. "Are we going to build a new world in sheer bluff and bombast?" Burns* [Chair of the Federal Reserve] *asked his diary.* (Farrell, 2017: 448)

There is no evidence that either Nixon or his Treasury Secretary (John Connally) had thought through the implications of the decision to kill off Bretton Woods or the potential consequences of doing so. They certainly had no successor arrangement in mind and were taken aback when their friends and allies reacted so strongly, leading to the Smithsonian Agreement.[9]

5.7   THE RISE OF THE RIGHT

Nancy MacLean's *Democracy in Chains: The Deep History of the Radical Right's Stealth Plan for America* (2017) describes how the current dominance of Neoliberal thinking in the Republican Party is largely due to the combination of the ideas of James M. Buchanan and the money and organising skills of Charles Koch. The 1970s economic crisis provided the opportunity. But even so it has taken a long time—and much manipulation of the media and politics—to achieve what most people would have thought impossible: getting people of modest means to vote for politicians who intend to reduce the social protections on which those people rely (see the review in the *New York Review of Books* by Diane Ravitch, 2017; see also Mayer, J. 2016).

As so often, it is the protagonists who give the game away. On page 283 MacLean quotes Nixon's Budget Director, David Stockman, on his failure, which was not for want of trying, to deliver the desired cuts in spending and taxes:

> *We can afford to be the arsenal of the free world and have our modest welfare state, too. The only thing we cannot afford to do is to continue pretending we do not have to fund it out of current taxation.*

MacLean shows how Buchanan's ideas originated in the need to protect white voters in Virginia after the Federal Government stepped up its desegregation efforts in the wake of the Supreme Court's 1955 ruling in Brown vs Board of Education. Vouchers to be used at private schools—first advocated by Milton Friedman, as we saw in Chap. 2—were seen as a means of enabling white children to be educated both separately from, and better than, black ones.

Higher education was another important site: slashing states' public budgets, raising tuition, ending needs-based scholarships (in favour of merit-based ones), limiting or curtailing academic tenure, reducing faculty governance, and undermining the liberal arts curriculum (cf. Newfield, 2011). MacLean observes that even though there was no empirical basis for Buchanan's work, universities were prepared to provide him with a home, 'as long as there was money on the table, they were not about to forgo it' (p. 203). Reputation was another attraction for less prestigious institutions so that the Rise of the Right is in part a symptom of the wider commercialisation of US academia (closely paralleled in Britain).[10]

MacLean observes that an important tactic was to reduce the voters' trust in politicians, already weakened by Johnson's lies over Vietnam as well as by Watergate and, later, Bill Clinton's philanderings. She also stresses the importance that Buchanan/Koch attached to changes to the constitution to further protect the wealthy and make their 'reforms' harder to reverse (with Chile again an example). We shall discuss in Chap. 7 the various ways in which conservative administrations have tried to ensure that their constitutional changes are hard to undo.[11]

5.8   FALSE CONSCIOUSNESS?

President Trump's 2017 tax cuts are a classic Neoliberal policy. As many have pointed out (e.g., Summers, 2017), the principal beneficiaries will be wealthy individuals and corporations and their stockholders (where the two sets of individuals are not the same).[12] Why then has there been such strong popular support for them? This seems indeed to be a classic case of Marx's 'false consciousness' (Engels, 1893), whereby a social group aims at objectives that do not benefit them. A number of case studies shed some light on this question.

The prototype is Thomas Frank's (2004) study of his home state, Kansas. Frank described how the Republican Right had managed to divert many middle- and lower-class workers away from economic to cultural issues and grievances (abortion, religion, gun control, gay marriage and evolution), with their ills blamed on a liberal intelligentsia represented in the media, academia, professional associations, etc.: people who wouldn't know how to load or clean a rifle.

The Democrats had helped this by focussing away from economic issues in the 1960s and 1970s, and then by adopting platforms in the 1990s and 2000s that were economically little different from the Republicans ('triangulation'). De-unionisation had played a key role because union members are more likely to be interested in economic issues and more liberal in stance (unions are also a channel for information about what is going on).

The beneficiaries were the 'money power' especially business. It is what he calls (2004: 79) 'the politics of self-delusion'. In Kansas, the political geography of social class has been turned upside down. This politics is ultimately class-based: it continues to dream its terrifying dreams of national decline, epic lawlessness and betrayal at the top regardless of what is going on in the world, which is actually seeing corporations cleaning up, with Kansas as a case in point. The Kansans vote for low taxes and cutting back the state even though Kansas relies heavily on government subsidies. However, the real shift to the Right was—in the 1990s—triggered by abortion. In short,

> *for decades Americans have experienced a populist uprising that only benefits the people it is supposed to be targeting* (Frank, 2004: 109).

By separating class from economics, the Right has built a Republican-friendly alternative for the disgruntled blue-collar American:

> *From Fox News and the Hoover Institute, and every newspaper in the land they sing the praises of the working man's red state virtues even while they pummel the working man's economic chances with outsourcing, new overtime rules, lousy health insurance and coercive new management techniques* (Frank, 2004: 151).

There was also a backlash against the 1960s and 1970s:

> *Recall for a moment the distinct sense of terminal crisis, of things coming apart, in the culture of those years; the endless hostage situation, the powerless president with his somber pessimism, the gasoline shortage, the crumbling cities, and, of course, the deliberately apocalyptic imagery of punk rock, which we in KC only knew from scaremongering news items.* (Frank, 2004: 146)

Finally, Frank emphasises the clarity of the conservative vision:

> *Everything fits together here; everything has its place; everyone ought to be happy in their station. The god of the market may not have much to offer you personally, but that doesn't change its divinity or blur the awesome clarity of the conservative vision.* (172)

In *Strangers in Their Own Land: Anger and Mourning on the American Right*, Arlie Russell Hochschild (2016) reports on interviews with families in or near Lake Charles in South West Louisiana. She uses environmental change and pollution—much of it very visible locally as a result of the operations of oil and chemicals companies—as the conversation trigger. She finds that what she describes as 'the shifting moral qualifications for the American Dream' had turned her interviewees into strangers in their own land, afraid, resentful, displaced and dismissed by the very people who were, they thought, 'cutting in line', the 'line' being the upward trajectory towards the Dream and the 'cutters-in' being immigrants, gay couples, etc. (religion is also important and race is never far away). The Federal Government is seen as the supplier and promoter of these cutters-in even though, as a poor state, Louisiana is heavily dependent on Federal subsidies, and even though Federal regulation is the best means of controlling the companies. This incidentally points up the way in which inequality breeds inequality. One major reason for this resentment is that as inequality has risen social mobility has fallen: the line is moving much more slowly.

In *The Politics of Resentment: Rural Consciousness in Wisconsin and the Rise of Scott Walker*, Katherine J Cramer (2016) describes the 'rural consciousness' that enabled Scott Walker to become Governor of Wisconsin in 2010 and destroy the public sector unions. Like Trump, Walker tapped into the resentment towards certain groups in society felt in this case by many outside the major population centres. Such consciousness has three main components: rural areas don't receive their fair share of decisionmaking power; rural areas are distinct from urban and suburban areas in their culture, values and lifestyles (which are not respected); and rural areas don't receive their fair share of resources. In other words, rural identity combines with a strong sense of allocative injustice. These attitudes matter because although country-dwellers only represent 15 per cent of the total US population, they are strongly attracted to the Republican Party and enabled the G.O.P to maintain control of the House (at least until 2018) and be competitive in rural elections.

Many of these themes are also found in Rana B. Khoury's acclaimed (2016) study of Ohio: the policy neglect of 'left behind' areas; the increasingly limited role of the labour unions; the losses of income and jobs as economic decline hits entire communities; the challenges for working women from the absence of maternity leave and affordable child care; the costs and inequalities in the education and health systems; the depredations of weakly regulated corporations in energy and agriculture; and the dominance of politics by the better off (even the Democrats depend on campaign contributions).

All of these studies emphasise the importance of cultural factors alongside economic ones in shaping political attitudes. We noted in Chap. 4 Richard Rorty's view that the Left's switch to 'identity politics' had left growing economic inequality to be exploited by the Right. In a classic account, William Berman (1998) also located the shift to the Right in the conservative reaction to the Great Society and the excesses of the Black Power movement which the Democrats were unable to handle. These are issues to which we shall return in Chaps. 6 and 7.

5.9 Conclusion

In this chapter and Chap. 4 we reviewed a wide range of explanations for the Neoliberal Turn. We shall offer our own thoughts in Chap. 7. But before that we need to look, in Chap. 6, at another piece of the jigsaw, the resurgence of authoritarian populism and the reasons for it.

Notes

1. The latter is a reference to the international role of the dollar. In a letter published in *The Guardian* on 12 August 2017 (p. 30), D.B.C. Reed quoted Enoch Powell as telling an audience in Cheltenham in 1968 that establishment moves were already afoot to convince the public (and the unions) that 'trade unions are responsible, wholly or partly, for rising prices and the falling value of money. It is really an astounding spectacle: the trade unions have clapped the handcuffs on to their own wrists, gone into the dock, and pleaded guilty to causing inflation'. Reed sees Nixon's August 1971 decision to let the dollar float (see below, A Superpower Transformed) as the main cause of the worldwide inflation and disruption that characterised most of the next decade (see also Conway, 2018 and Note 9). I have unfortunately been unable to contact Reed.
2. For Neoliberalism's willingness (and need) to mobilise the state, see Chap. 4, Note 1, and Chap. 7.
3. In a 2019 article, Aditya Chakrabortty argued that the 'Thatcher experiment' had 'pretty well failed':

    > *Four decades after she took power, 38% of working-age households now take more from the state in benefits, health and education than they pay back in taxes. Wealth in Britain is now so concentrated that the head of the Institute for Fiscal Studies believes "inheritance is probably the most important factor in determining a person's overall wealth since Victorian times".*

    As noted in Chap. 1, the Johnson Government's 'levelling up' policy (Department for Levelling Up, Housing and Communities, 2022) is essentially an attempt to reduce these regional disparities (see Chap. 7).

4. Mike Conczal's *Freedom from the Market* (2018) is a very useful review of the ways in which the US has historically managed to balance the needs of society with the market.

5. Prasad makes an interesting observation about the ability of politicians in adversarial systems to exploit secondary issues, often falsely. Political 'demagoguery' arises where a politician mobilises opinion on what most people would see as a secondary issue, and where the claims made are demonstrably false. Political entrepreneurship arises where only the first condition applies (Prasad, 2006: 36). The emphasis placed on immigration in the Brexit Leave (and Trump) campaigns would appear to be excellent examples of such demagoguery, and even Brexit itself: Simon Kuper noted in the *Financial Times* in 2019 that according to polling by Ipsos Mori, in the decade to 2015, typically fewer than 10 per cent of Britons had named the EU as 'one of the most important issues facing the country'. Even in the 2015 election, with the conservatives pledging a referendum if they won, only 6 per cent said the EU was the main issue.

6. According to current OECD statistics, of the Organisation's 38 members and associates in 2020, only South Africa and Costa Rica had a higher proportion than the US of people whose income fell below the poverty line (with the poverty line defined as half the median income of the total population). (Retrieved 13 January 2022 from https://data.oecd.org/inequality/poverty-rate.htm). Of course, consumption is the main driver of both the American and British economies.

7. As a sometime union official, Reagan could see that tax cuts could appeal to working-class voters:

> *Those who belong to unions … are preoccupied with what used to be called middle class problems: property taxes, interest rates on loans, the price of a car or recreational vehicle. The no longer identify with the aging New Deal agenda of social activism.* (Sam Hurst, The New Democratic Coalition *Los Angeles Times* 22 February 1981, quoted in Prasad, 2018: 90)

8. According to an analysis of IMF data by Mark Dixon and Patrick Clark of Solent University, every major OECD country increased the share of government expenditure in GDP between 1950 and the mid-1970s. There were further increases subsequently. However, certain countries remained bigger public spenders than others: levels of government expenditure have been highest in France and Sweden (although the latter has fallen spectacularly since the early 1990s); low in Japan and the US; and middling in the UK and Germany. The data source is https://www.imf.org/external/datamapper/exp@FPP/USA/FRA/JPN/GBR/SWE/DEU.

9. In an article in *The Guardian* in August 2021 Larry Elliott argued that Nixon's decision to break the dollar-gold link (which was welcomed as a liberalising decision by Milton Friedman and other Neoliberal economists) opened the Pandora's Box of 'volatile financial markets, geopolitical tension, inflated asset prices underwritten by low interest rates and QE, and where trust in central banks is starting to wear a bit thin'.

10. A more recent book by Ralph Wilson and Isaac Kamola (2021) describes how the Koch network is trying to foment 'campus wars' around alleged threats to 'free speech'.

11. There does not appear to be a comparable study of the rise of the Right in Britain, but Richard Cockett's (1994) book *Thinking the Unthinkable* remains essential reading for the development of conservative thought up to the 1980s (see also Dorey, 2011). There are clear parallels in the lowering of trust in politicians in Britain which arguably began with the MPs' expenses scandal in 2009 and has culminated for the moment in Boris Johnson's 'partygate'.

12. A widely accepted analysis by the independent Tax Policy Center (2018) found that the Tax Cuts and Jobs Act would reduce taxes on average for all income groups in both 2018 and 2025. But in general, higher-income households would receive larger average tax cuts as a percentage of after-tax income, with the largest cuts as a share of income going to taxpayers in the 95th–99th percentiles of the income distribution. On average, in 2027 taxes would change little for lower- and middle-income groups but would decrease for higher-income groups. Robert Kuttner's (2018: 312) verdict seems just:

> As the details of his actual policies sank in, he was increasingly revealed (and reviled) as an ordinary Republican plutocrat trying to disguise his corporate agenda with faux-populist rantings, scapegoating foreigners, and embracing racists.

References

Authers, J. (2017, September 23–24). The next crisis is coming and investors need to prepare. *Financial Times.*

Beatty, C., & Fothergill, S. (2016). *Jobs, welfare and austerity: How the destruction of industrial Britain casts a shadow over present-day public finances.* Centre for Regional Economic and Social Research, Sheffield Hallam University.

Beatty, C., Fothergill, S., & Gore, T. (2017). *The real level of unemployment 2017.* Centre for Regional Economic and Social Research, Sheffield Hallam University.

Bell, D. N. F., & Blanchflower, D. G. (2018). *The lack of wage growth and the NAIRU.* National Bureau of Economic Research Working Paper 24502. NBER.

Berman, W. C. (1998). *America's right turn: From Nixon to Clinton* (2nd ed.). Johns Hopkins University Press.

Cockett, R. (1994). *Thinking the unthinkable: Think-tanks and the economic counter-revolution, 1931-1983.* Harper Collins.

Conway, E. (2018, November 2). A warning from the saviour of free markets. *The Times.*

Coutts, K., & Gudgin, G. (2015). *The macroeconomic impact of liberal economic policies in the UK.* Centre for Business Research, Judge Business School, University of Cambridge.

Cramer, K. J. (2016). *The politics of resentment: Rural consciousness and the rise of Scott Walker.* Chicago University Press.

Department for Levelling Up, Housing and Communities. (2022). *Levelling up the United Kingdom.* Department for Levelling Up, Housing and Communities.

Dorey, P. (2011). *British Conservatism: The politics and philosophy of inequality.* Tauris.

Drutman, L. (2015). *The business of America is lobbying: How corporations became politicized and politics became more corporate.* Oxford University Press.

Engels, F. (1893, July 14). *Letter to Franz Mehring.* International Publishers. Retrieved October 6, 2018, from https://www.marxists.org/archive/marx/works/1893/letters/93_07_14.htm.

Farrell, J. A. (2017). *Richard Nixon: The life.* Scribe.

Frank, T. (2004). *What's the matter with Kansas? How Conservatives won the heart of America.* Picador.

Goldin, C., & Margo, R. A. (1991). *The great compression: The wage structure in the United States at mid-century.* National Bureau of Economic Research Working Paper No. 3817. NBER.

Greenspan, A., & Wooldridge, A. (2018). *Capitalism in America: A history.* Penguin Press/Allen Press.

Hacker, J. S., & Pierson, P. (2010). *Winner-take-all-politics: How Washington made the rich richer and turned its back on the middle class.* Simon and Schuster.

Hacker, J. S., & Pierson, P. (2016). *American Amnesia: How the war on government led us to forget what made America prosper.* Simon and Schuster.

Henry, S. G. B. (2014). The Coalition's economic strategy: Has it made a bad thing worse? *Economic Outlook, 38*(2), 14–20.

Hochschild, A. R. (2016). *Strangers in their own land: Anger and mourning on the American right.* Free Press.

Katz, A. (2015). *The influence machine: The US Chamber of Commerce and the corporate capture of American life.* Spiegel and Grau.

Khoury, R. B. (2016). *As Ohio goes: Life in the post-recession nation.* Kent State University Press.

Krieger, J. (1986). *Reagan, Thatcher and the politics of decline.* Oxford University Press.

Kuttner, R. (2018). *Can democracy survive global capitalism?* W.W.Norton.

Lafer, G. (2017). *The one per cent solution: How corporations are remaking America one state at a time.* Cornell University Press.

Martin, I. W. (2008). *The permanent tax revolt: How the property tax transformed American politics.* Stanford University Press.

Mayer, T. (1999). *Monetary policy and the great inflation in the US. The Federal Reserve and the failure of macroeconomic policy 1965-1979.* Edward Elgar.

Mayer, J. (2016). *Dark money: The hidden history of the billionaires behind the rise of the radical right.* Scribe.

Newfield, C. (2011). *Unmaking the public university: The forty-year assault on the middle class.* Harvard University Press.

Prasad, M. (2006). *The politics of free markets.* University of Chicago Press.

Prasad, M. (2011). *The land of too much: American abundance and the paradox of poverty.* Harvard University Press.

Prasad, M. (2018). *Starving the beast: Ronald Reagan and the tax cut revolution.* Russell Sage.

Ravitch, D. (2017, December 7). Big money rules. *The New York Review of Books.*

Reid, J., Burns, N., & Chanda, S. (2017). *Long-term asset return study: An ever changing world.* Deutsche Bank AG. http://www.tramuntalegria.com/wp-content/uploads/2017/09/Long-Term-Asset-Return-Study-The-Next-Financial-Crisis-db.pdf.

Sargent, D. J. (2015). *A superpower transformed: The remaking of American foreign relations in the 1970s.* Oxford University Press.

Stein, J. (2010). *Pivotal decade: How the United States traded factories for finance in the seventies.* Yale University Press.

Summers, L. (2017, November 6). A Republican tax plan that will help the rich and harm growth. *Financial Times.* Retrieved November 6, 2017, from https://www.ft.com/content/5c0be71a-bf2a-11e7-823b-ed31693349d3.

Tax Policy Center. (2018). *Analysis of the tax cuts and jobs act.* Retrieved November 7, 2018, from https://www.taxpolicycenter.org/feature/analysis-tax-cuts-and-jobs-act.

Wilson, R., & Kamola, I. (2021). *Free speech and Koch money: Manufacturing a campus culture war.* Pluto Press.

Wren-Lewis, S. (2018). *The lies we were told: Politics, economics and Brexit.* Bristol University Press.

CHAPTER 6

Authoritarian Populism and its Sources

Abstract There has been a rise in authoritarian populism (AP)—authoritarian values cloaked in populist rhetoric—in many advanced Western countries including not only the UK and the US. However, there is no consensus about the causes. A survey of recent writings suggests that the phenomenon has both cultural and economic drivers, but that an important contributory factor has been the inability of the democratic party system to cope with the demands made on it since the late-1970s. This chapter is in two parts. The first part introduces recent theories about the meaning of populism. The second discusses some recent explanations for the rise of AP with particular reference to the Brexit vote and the election of President Trump (both 2016).

Keywords Authoritarianism • Democracy • Liberalism • Political parties • Populism

*The policy reversals that began in the 1970s and intensified in the 1980s restored classical **economic** liberalism via globalization, at great cost to **political** liberalism* (Kuttner, 2018: 266, original author's emphases).

Populism is an illiberal democratic response to undemocratic liberalism (Mudde, 2015).

© The Author(s), under exclusive license to Springer Nature   85
Switzerland AG 2022
R. Brown, *The Conservative Counter-Revolution in Britain and
America 1980–2020*,
https://doi.org/10.1007/978-3-031-09142-1_6

> *The basic idea behind populism … is that democracy has been stolen from the people by the elites* (Runciman, *2019*: 65).

> *Trump … has tapped into America's deep historical mistrust of unchecked markets, and poisoned it with racial and sexist appeals, to create the mirage of a better future—for some. The concrete results are tax cuts for the rich, increased precarity for workers, and aggressive policing for the rest* (Konczal, *2021*: 186).

> *The United States remains threatened by plutocratic populism, a toxic combination of culture war on the ground and the ultrawealthy trying to capture the political system at the top* (Mueller, *2021b*).

6.1   What is Populism?

There does not seem to be any generally agreed definition. A 2017 Bridgewater study of the characteristics of populist leaders in the 1930s and between the wars (Dalio et al., 2017) found that they took advantage of poor economic conditions, an uneven recovery from which the elite were seen as prospering, political squabbling and ineffectual policy making, and a feeling that foreigners or others were threatening their values and way of life. These leaders,

- *Aligned themselves with 'the people' or 'the common man'*
- *Were anti-establishment and attacked the current ruling interests*
- *Sought to undermine those elites in favour of others*
- *Were strongly nationalist and held national unity as a key aim*
- *Detested the debate and disagreement inherent in democracy*
- *Tended to be anti-international, anti-global trade and anti-immigrant*

(Dalio et al., 2017: 5).

There is a substantial overlap here with the analysis in Jan Werner-Mueller's, 2016 *What is Populism?* Mueller describes populists as being critical of elites, antipluralist (they and they alone represent 'the people') and exclusionary (populists treat their opponents as 'enemies of the people' and seek to exclude them from politics altogether). In Government, populism exhibits three main characteristics: attempts to hijack the state apparatus, corruption and mass clientelism (trading material benefits or bureaucratic favours for political support from citizens who become the populists' clients).

Mueller argues that populism makes a certain kind of moral claim:

> *Populism ... is a **particular moralistic imagination of politics**, a way of perceiving the political world that sets a morally pure and fully united – but ultimately fictional – people against elites who are deemed corrupt or in some other way morally inferior.* (Mueller, 2016: 19–20, original author's emphasis)[1]

Finally, there is the irony that, in power:

> *Populism ... brings about, reinforces, or offers another variety of the very exclusion and usurpation of the state that it most opposes in the reigning establishment it seeks to replace. What the 'old establishment' or 'corrupt, immoral elites' supposedly have always done, the populists will also end up doing – only, one would have thought, without guilt and without a supposedly democratic justification.* (Mueller, 2016: 49)

The change from one elite to another may not even involve much actual change. In a more recent book, Mueller notes that with the possible exception of Italy,

> *until today, in no Western country has a right-wing populist authoritarian party or politician come to power without the collaboration of established conservative elites.* (Mueller, 2021a: xi)[2]

On the basis of an historical review of populism in early nineteenth-century Britain, imperial Germany and the US since 1918, Barry Eichengreen (2018) observes that populism flourishes most when economic insecurity exposes the divergent interests of people and elites. The key traits are anti-establishmentarianism, authoritarianism and nativism. Populists depict politics as an elite conspiracy that produces results inimical to the interests of 'the people'. Weak economic growth, rising inequality, falling social mobility and increasing insecurity of employment all fuel populism. The key remedies are therefore the revival of economic growth and security and tackling the dysfunctionality of the political system.

Taking into account the US experience of the 1890s as well as more recent times, David Runciman (2019: 67) identifies four requirements: economic distress, technological change, growing inequality and an absence of war. He notes that the appeal of modern democracies lies in their ability to deliver long-term benefits (stability, prosperity and peace) while providing individual citizens with a voice: benefits plus recognition. But,

> *contemporary authoritarians have tried to learn the lessons of the twentieth century like anyone else. They offer the other half of what democracy can provide, but not the whole. In place of personal dignity plus collective benefits, they promise personal benefits plus collective dignity* (2019: 171).

6.2   What Explains the Recent Surge in Authoritarian Populism (AP)?

The Bridgewater analysis shows that support for parties/candidates in the West who make attacking the political/corporate establishment their key political cause is higher now than at any time since the late-1930s.[3] Why? Broadly, five sets of theories are considered here:

1. those that emphasise cultural factors;
2. those that emphasise economic factors;
3. those that combine both sets of factors;
4. those that see the problem as lying in the way that conventional political parties have failed to cope with external demands, especially those arising from globalisation and technological change, both sets of demands being channelled and strengthened through strong market-based policies;
5. those that see the problem in terms of 'political marketing'.

6.3   Cultural Theories

Norris and Inglehart (2019) attributed the rise of AP to the reaction of older, less well-educated and less cosmopolitan individuals and groups to the socially liberal values increasingly espoused across society, and especially by younger generations, since the 1960s/70s, a 'cultural backlash' that has been exploited by ruthless demagogues like Trump and Johnson taking advantage of 'winner-takes-all', 'first-past-the-post', majoritarian electoral systems (as well as the enormous 'reach' of modern social media). Whilst Norris and Englehart certainly acknowledge the importance of economic grievances, they argue that AP is chiefly driven by cultural and identity factors: for a very similar analysis, see Curtice (2016) and Stoller (2016).

A 2017 post-Brexit survey by Maria Sobolewska and Robert Ford (2018) focussed on attitudes towards immigration and whether it benefits Britain. The authors found that the answers to these questions gave a strong indication of the respondent's view on Brexit. Those who thought that equal opportunities for ethnic minorities had gone too far voted heavily Leave, whereas those who felt that equal opportunities had not gone far enough were more likely to have voted Remain. The authors commented that while Britain had not yet seen the 'culture wars' over identity, diversity and legacies of prejudice of the kind that had bedevilled US politics almost since the Revolution (and of which we were all reminded by the George Floyd affair in 2020), the robust association of views about ethnic equality and votes in the EU referendum could be a warning signal of how our politics might be changing.

In a more recent (2020) book, the authors argue that three main developments have led to a clear cultural divide: educational expansion (which has shifted the country's educational profile), mass immigration and rising ethnic diversity (which has transformed the typical experience of a young person growing up in Britain), and the opening up of a major generational divide in the electorate. These are of course not unique to Britain, as analysis of voting patterns in the US presidential election demonstrates (e.g., Jennings, 2020).[4]

Boris Johnson's August 2020 criticism of the BBC for initially intending to change the traditional Last Night of the Proms renditions of 'Rule Britannia' and 'Land of Hope and Glory'—ironically, an action taken by the BBC to comply with his own Government's Covid guidance to the performing arts sector about choirs—suggests that he recognises the political advantages of a culture war where he can persuade voters that he is on their side while a cosmopolitan, London-centric, 'woke' Labour Party is not (Behr, 2020). Nesrine Malik (2020) even claims:

> *Culture war skirmishes are no longer a sideshow to our politics, they are our politics. They are how rightwing electoral prospects are now advanced: not through policies or promises of a better life, but by fostering a sense of threat, a fantasy that something profoundly pure and British is constantly at risk of extinction.*

The Government's 'war' against the BBC, culminating for the moment in the Culture Secretary's (Nadine Dorries's) threat to abolish the licence fee (Clinton, 2022), is a continuation of this pattern, as it is increasing willingness to intervene in board appointments to major arts and cultural bodies (e.g., Gray, 2021).

In a 2016 blog entitled 'It's NOT the economy, stupid: Brexit as a story of personal values', Eric Kaufmann compared data from the US presidential primaries and the Brexit referendum campaign. Kaufmann sought 'predictors' that would indicate whether the voter was pro- or anti-Brexit/Trump. He found that the top predictor was attitude towards the death penalty, followed by attitudes towards immigration and party allegiance. Income and class ('left-behindness'), age and education status were all much weaker. 'Authoritarian/liberal' or 'order/openness' were the best ways of encapsulating these very different ideas of how to live.[5]

Kaufmann linked the differences to work by Cultural Dynamics (2016). The pro-Leave/Trump attitudes were within a 'Settler' category, for whom belonging, certainty, roots and safety are paramount. Such people are disproportionately opposed to immigration (irrespective of whether their area has actually been impacted by immigration, never mind the irony of the fact that both the American and British economies were enriched through the enslavement of African immigrants). By contrast, those who were oriented to success and display ('Promoters'), and those who prioritised expressive individualism and cultural equality ('Prospectors') voted Remain.

In a 2014 article, John Holmwood noted that, apart from Britain, the countries that constitute the 'liberal cluster' (the US, Australia, New Zealand and Canada) were all 'settler capitalists'. While Britain was not literally a 'settler capitalist' country, it was a country that (preeminently) settled and provided settlers, 'thereby creating interconnections with settler capitalist economies and shaping its own political economy through colonial encounters' (Holmwood, 2014: 613).

A 2018 *Guardian* study (Walker, 2018) found attitudes to Islam, alongside attitudes to immigration and multiculturalism, to be a major differentiating factor. This also had a geographical dimension. All of the 100 areas where people were most likely to oppose immigration were in towns or on the outskirts of cities, with 93 of them in the Midlands or North. In contrast, the 100 areas most linked to a 'confident multicultural population' were all in major cities or close to universities, with 90% of them located within a few hundred metres of a university. Lastly, an

attempt to identify centres of strongly anti-Muslim or far-right senti-
ment—by mapping the locations of people who signed an on-line petition
for the release from prison of the anti-Islam activist Tommy Robinson—
found a strong correlation with the deprived towns associated with Brexit
and more general opposition to immigration.[6]

Some commentators (e.g., Niven, 2020) indeed discern in the voting
patterns for Trump and Brexit a growing gulf between the major cities and
the rest of the country, with the younger and better educated migrating to
the cities and leaving their 'home' areas behind (in more than one sense).
This may be another instance of Bill Bishop's 'sorting'. It is not confined
to the US/UK. In a 2019 *Observer* report, Julian Coman noted that whilst
Milan had voted for the Democratic Party in the recent elections, the rest
of Lombardy voted for Matteo Salvini's far-right Northern League.

Danny Dorling has pointed out (2018: 69–72) that 52% of the people
who voted Leave lived in the South. Fifty-nine percent were middle class
(A, B or C1). The proportion of Leave voters who were of the two lowest
social classes (D or E) was just 24%. The Leave voters amongst the middle
classes were crucial to the final result because the middle class constituted
two-thirds of those who actually voted. Similarly, Simon Kuper (2020a)
notes that according to the American National Election Study, about two-
thirds of Trump voters in 2016 had household incomes above $50,000
(then about the US average). In the Netherlands, two-thirds of supporters
of the far-right Thierry Baudet are moderately or highly educated.

A 2021 study by UK in a Changing Europe found that almost half of
Brexit supporters were 'affluent Eurosceptics' who wanted further investment in the police, the NHS and care workers. Encouraged by the Leave
campaign—'£350 million each week for the NHS'—they believed that
Brexit would free up the necessary funding.

William Davies (2020) argues that Leavers (and supporters of No Deal)
combined

> *those who have already accumulated assets over their lives plus some who are
> unlikely to ever do so. Remain voters consisted of those who still feel … that they
> could make financialisation work for them, either because they're young or
> because they're still benefitting from asset appreciation.* (Davies, 2020: 39)

The British Election Study (2016) thought that the key to understanding the Brexit vote was the individual voter's 'locus of control'. Those
with an 'external' locus of control (feeling themselves helpless to control

their lives) were much more likely to vote Leave than those who felt themselves to be largely responsible for what happens to them. Distance from centres of political power could be a factor here.

Finally, as we noted in Chap. 5, cultural factors have also been prominent in several recent studies of 'left behind' social groups in rural America. But even there, economic factors like the loss of jobs and/or secure employment have also played a part. J.D. Vance's best-selling *Hillbilly Elegy* (2016), a memoir of a struggling Appalachian family's life, also deals with the employment problems being faced by such poor white groups in present-day America.

What all these groups feel—and many Trump and Leave supporters share—is a concern about the continuity of their identity and way of life. This is even above money or social status. As discussed in Chap. 5, this may be the phenomenon of 'false consciousness' first identified by Marx and Engels (1893), termed 'the politics of self-delusion' by Thomas Frank (2004), explored most recently by Jonathan Haidt (2013) and exploited most heavily by Trump (winning over the Rust Belt in 2016) and Johnson (winning Red Wall seats in 2019).

6.4   ECONOMICS

We now turn to economic theories for the rise of AP.

An edited 2013 book (Parker, 2013)—also drawing heavily on UK-US evidence—draws attention to the role of the 'squeezed middle'. These are intermediate households that have for long suffered stagnant wages, greater employment insecurity, sharply rising costs as state and employer support for health and pensions has been cut back, poorer access to home ownership, and lower social mobility. They are suffering from the breakdown in the longstanding societal bargain whereby, if you do your part, you can expect a decent standard of living, for both you and your offspring, in return. A 5 February 2017 letter in *The Observer* by David Redshaw nicely encapsulated this:

> *Before Mrs Thatcher, many middle-class couples existed on one income, the women not working or only going back when their children were older, while many working-class women put in five half-days a week. Rents were controlled, public transport was cheap and plentiful and work was more secure, with the employer shouldering more of the national insurance costs.*

Margaret Thatcher hit us with the perfect storm, and there wasn't a minimum wage until 1997, after several years of Thatcher and Nigel Lawson's housing policies had made it necessary. It's gone up most years since then, struggling vainly to keep up with house-price generated inflation.[7]

Another major study (Joseph Rowntree Foundation, 2016) is a classic statement of the 'left behind' thesis:

Groups in Britain who have been 'left behind' by rapid economic change and feel cut adrift from the mainstream consensus were the most likely to support Brexit. These voters face a 'double whammy'. While their lack of qualifications put them at a significant disadvantage in the modern economy, they are also being further marginalised in society by the lack of opportunities in their low-skilled communities.

A Resolution Foundation study (Finch, 2016) identified those 'just managing' as the six million working-age households which get most of their income from employment but who are amongst the poorest half of households. This group has suffered pronounced degradation since the 2008 crash. This has been accompanied by a significant rise in the cost of living, especially in the cost of housing. So they are squeezed at both ends. In fact, the rise in housing costs since the turn of the century was the equivalent of an extra 14p on the basic rate of income tax.

An earlier Resolution Foundation blog (Bell, 2016) drew attention to the fact that real average weekly earnings (average weekly earnings adjusted for CPI inflation) were then still £20 below the pre-crisis peak of £490. There was a clear correlation between the share of the pro-Brexit vote and hourly earnings by local authority area (cf. Bell & Machin, 2016).

There are some parallels here with the argument in Azmanova (2019) that, together, globalisation, technological change and reduced social safety nets have extended to previously successful labour market insiders the conditions of uncertainty and instability that were previously experienced only by the less fortunate. This development has gone beyond inequality although inequality of wealth in particular is a major part of it.

A 2017 study (Antonucci et al.) looked at the role such intermediate households might have played in the Brexit vote. The conclusion, based upon individual-level data from a post-Brexit survey based on the British Election Study, was that

1. voting Leave is (or was) associated more with intermediate levels of education (high grades GCSE, A level) than with low or absent education, in particular when in the presence of a perceived declining economic position.
2. Brexiters hold distinct psycho-social features of malaise due to declining economic conditions, especially that of feeling left out of society.
3. voting Leave was associated with self-identification as middle class, rather than as working class. Intermediate levels of income were not more likely to vote for Remain than low-income groups.

A more recent analysis (McCurdy et al., 2020) found that the Labour Party's former political heartlands in the North, Midlands and Wales had suffered from a tougher squeeze on wages and slower jobs growth than the rest of Britain over the previous decade. The 50 seats covered in the study were nevertheless closer to the national average for household income and demography and were better off, than other labour strongholds. Average incomes in the new Red Wall seats were somewhat lower than in the average Tory seat, but still above other Labour constituencies.

Yet another study, by the Institute for the Future of Work (Pissarides et al., 2019), found a close match between parts of the UK affected by automation and those voting for Leave. Similarly, Westlake (2016) suggests that support for Brexit might be a reaction to the underlying structural economic shift from tangibles to intangibles and the advantage this gives to 'symbolic analysts' who can make sense of abstract concepts, argue and enforce claims (i.e., the more highly educated). A 2018 analysis by Warwick economists (Fetzer et al., 2018) estimated that because the Coalition Government's austerity policies disproportionately affected the most deprived areas, without those policies the Leave vote would have been nearly ten points lower, giving a clear victory to Remain. A report in *The Times* (Wright, 2019) quoted the principal author:

The swing voters who decided the referendum were not diehard Eurosceptics. They were concerned about public goods and services and feeling the impact of austerity policies. If it hadn't been for austerity, more of these marginal voters would have voted the other way and the referendum wouldn't have turned out the way it did.

It would be very interesting to know whether David Cameron took the effects of austerity on these voters into account in his decision to promise an EU referendum (we can probably guess the answer).

A 2016 analysis of educational disadvantage by Sam Freedman found a clear association between poor school results and a high percentage of Leave votes. In Leave areas, just 29% of those in receipt of Free School Meals (a generally recognised indicator of disadvantage) achieved the five good GCSEs in English and Maths usually accepted as a basic educational standard, whereas in Remain areas the percentage was 46. The underlying reasons for the discrepancy were economic. Hackney actually has a higher proportion of pupils eligible for free school meals than Blackpool, but it is in the heart of the capital and is surrounded by universities and multinational companies. Freedman remarked that if 'levelling-up' is to occur, places like Blackpool will need strong economic incentives for companies to invest, high-quality social housing and adequate mental health services as well as well-funded schools able to attract the best teachers and educational leaders. This reinforces much other research (e.g., Centre for Social Investigation, 2020) which shows that it is not so much educational opportunities that need to be levelled up as the economic and social conditions that constrain those opportunities, as already noted in Chap. 2.

Finally, Paul Arbair (2016) acknowledges the force of the 'winners and losers from globalisation' thesis but argues that the real reason for the rise of populism is the long slow disappearance of economic growth:

> Businesses assume that their revenues and profits should expand, consumers that their purchasing power and living standards ought to go up, governments that their tax revenues will naturally climb over time. Lenders and borrowers assume that borrowers will be able to repay their debts and businesses to pay dividends. All make their spending and investment decisions, as well as related long-term financial commitments, on the basis of widely shared assumptions that the economy will grow. Voters, in turn, assume that political leaders will maximise growth and use its proceeds to constantly increase societal welfare. To a certain extent, economic growth has come to form part of the Western social contract, and its absence is perceived by some as a breach by government of its tacit contractual obligations.

The decline of economic growth has in turn led to a loss of confidence in existing political systems: 'political institutions maintain a semblance of functionality but are getting increasingly incapable of solving the major issues facing complex societies'. This makes many voters easy meat for apparent enemies of the political status quo: for a similar analysis, see Techau (2016) and Luce (2017). Of course, as we saw in Chap. 3, lower economic growth has been one of the principal impacts of the Neoliberal Turn.

6.5   Culture + Economics

Several analyses conflate the economic and cultural factors. Will Jennings (2016) saw the Brexit referendum as a battle between the 'cosmopolitans' (Labour and LibDem supporters, young educated people and professionals, with *Guardian* readers the most Europhile of all) and those who have had a much worse deal from an increasingly global economy and the decline of the manufacturing base, but who are also suspicious of social and cultural change. Similarly, the influential study of the Brexit vote by Matthew Goodwin and Oliver Heath (2016):

> *The vote for Brexit was anchored predominantly, albeit not exclusively, in areas of the country that are filled with pensioners, low skilled and less well educated blue-collar workers and citizens who have been pushed to the margins not only by the economic transformation of the country, but by the values that have come to dominate a more socially liberal media and political class. In this respect, the vote for Brexit was delivered by the 'left behind' – social groups that are united by a general sense of insecurity, pessimism and marginalisation, who do not feel as though elites, whether in Brussels or Westminster, represent their interests and genuinely empathise with their intense angst about rapid change.*

A more recent (2020) study of the 2019 Election by the same authors describes why so many low-income voters turned away from Labour, especially in the Red Wall constituencies. They argue that Labour needs to reconnect with these voters not only through economic policies but also by tapping into concerns about Britain's place in the world, immigration, law and order, and rapid social change. This is also the message of Sebastian Payne's, 2021 best seller *Broken Heartlands: A Journey Through Labour's Lost England*.

Yet another Resolution Foundation commentary (Clarke, 2016) found that the Brexit vote was driven by a mix of living standards, demographic and cultural factors (this time covering variables such as employment, household income, education, views on immigration and their position on a 'liberal-authoritarian' scale).

A 2017 *Financial Times* analysis based on a detailed Ipsos/Mori survey of 4000 voters (Burn-Murdoch, 2017) found that education levels, attitudes towards immigration and the rural-urban divide stood out as the strongest dividing lines when all groups were considered; factors such as age, social class and party allegiance had a more nuanced effect on voters' behaviour. The study identified six groups: 'British values' Leavers (10% of the population); working-class Leavers (15%); moderate Leavers (18%); disengaged Remainers (16%); young, urban Remainers (11%) and older, liberal Remainers (15%).

A 2017 BBC analysis of votes from nearly half of the local authorities that counted referendum ballots (Rosenbaum, 2017) found that local results were chiefly determined by a combination of education, age and ethnicity. People with lower qualifications were significantly more liable to vote Leave, as were older voters. Ethnic minority voters were more likely to vote Remain although in parts of London some Asian populations voted Leave.

Also in 2017, Geoffrey Evans and James Tilley found a clear connection between an area's social make-up and the percentage of Leavers/Remainers. In the 77 council areas where more than 30% of people were in working-class jobs, the Leave vote was more than 20% higher than in the 62 areas with less than 20% in working-class jobs. There was more than a 20% gap in the Leave vote between the 62 areas with less than 20% graduates, and the 99 areas with more than 30% graduates. There were also huge differences in vote choice by education: while 72% of those with no qualifications voted Leave, only 35% of graduates did so.

6.6   The Future of Political Parties

The conclusion that in trying to explain AP we need to take account of both economic and cultural factors is reinforced by some reflection on three more recent books.

In *Caste: The Origins of Our Discontents* (2020), Isabelle Wilkerson sees racism in the US as an aspect of a caste system: a society-wide system of social stratification characterised by notions like hierarchy, inclusion and exclusion, and purity. But one can broaden the argument. Many of those who have supported Trump and Johnson are threatened not only by economic changes; there is also the threat posed by social liberalism's removal of the barriers to the advancement of hitherto disadvantaged groups and the consequent threat to their middle- or lower-middle-class status.[8,9]

In *The Tyranny of Merit: What's Become of the Common Good?* Michael J Sandel (2020) draws attention to two developments that have rendered liberal democracy vulnerable to market-based globalisation: the technocratic way of conceiving the public good and the meritocratic way of labelling 'winners' and 'losers'. The former is bound up with the faith that markets are the primary instrument for achieving the public good. The latter—the conviction that a just society distributes income and wealth roughly in proportion to what people deserve—pronounces a harsh verdict on the losers and makes them feel humiliation and resentment against actual or perceived 'elites' (for an argument on similar lines, see Goodhart, 2020). Bukodi and Goldthorpe (2021) find some evidence for an association between meritocracy and populism.

In the 2016 study of populism already referred to, Jan-Werner Mueller draws on some work by Bickerton and Invenizzi Accetti (2015) to argue that both populism and technocracy are responses to the failure of the conventional party system to deal with popular grievances. Party democracy is here seen as having two main features:

> *The mediation of social conflict through the institution of the political party, understood as a means for the articulation of particular interests into comprehensive – although competing – conceptions of the common good; and the idea that the specific conception of the common good that ought to prevail and therefore be translated into public policy is the one that is simultaneously constructed and identified through the democratic procedures of parliamentary deliberation and electoral competition, which is often but not always based on majority rule.* (Bickerton & Invenizzi Accetti, 2015: 8)

In short, political mediation and a procedural conception of political legitimacy.

So far from being opposites to one another, populism and technocracy are seen as complementary alternatives to party democracy: technocracy holds that there is only one correct policy solution, populism claims that there is only one authentic will of the people. In other words, each legitimises the belief that there is no real room for disagreement (and therefore no need for organisations that foment it).[10]

There is a clear overlap here with Sandel's argument that technocracy, as the summa of a meritocratic society, is one of the things that has made politics more partisan:

What the technocratic discourse and the shouting matches have in common is a failure to engage in a substantive way with the moral convictions that animate democratic citizens; neither cultivates the habit of reasoning together about competing conceptions of justice and the common good. (Sandel, 2020: 108)

But where do the grievances that give rise to the shouting matches come from, and what is the evidence that they are stressing existing party democracy?

As already discussed, Sandel (2020: 19–22) links the technocratic way of conceiving the public good to Neoliberalism:

The technocratic conception of politics is bound up with a faith in markets – not necessarily unfettered laissez-faire capitalism, but the broader belief that market mechanisms are the primary instruments for achieving the public good. This way of thinking about politics is technocratic in the sense that it drains public discourse of substantive moral argument and treats ideologically contestable questions as if they were matters of economic efficiency, the province of experts.

The weakening of party democracy was the central theme of the late Peter Mair's *Ruling the Void: The Hollowing of Western Democracy* (published in 2013 but based on work on European parties between 2007 and 2011).

Mair's argument was that parties were failing in two ways.

First, parties are increasingly failing in their capacity to engage ordinary citizens, who are voting in smaller numbers than before and with less sense of partisan consistency, and are also increasingly reluctant to commit themselves to parties, whether in terms of identification or membership. In this sense, citizens are withdrawing from conventional political involvement.

Second, the parties can no longer adequately serve as a base for the activities and status of their own leaders, who increasingly direct their ambitions towards external public institutions and draw their resources from them.

Parties are failing, in other words, as a result of a process of mutual withdrawal or abandonment, whereby citizens retreat into private life or into more specialized often ad hoc forms of representation, while the party leaderships retreat into the institutions, drawing their terms of reference ever more readily from their roles as governors or public-office holders. Parties are failing because the zone of engagement – the traditional world of party democracy where citizens interacted with and felt a sense of attachment to their political leaders – is being evacuated. (Mair, 2013: 16)

Mair did not give a clear explanation for these changes.

On the one hand, he mentioned the declining ability of national governments (and therefore national parties) to be able to determine economic and other policies in the light of global economic developments. This is a reference to Ruggie's (1982) 'end of embedded liberalism' that we covered in Chap. 4. Elsewhere, he drew attention to the growing difficulty of appealing to and relying upon collective values and interests in a world of individualisation and particularism. So it always comes back to Neoliberalism!

On the other hand, Mair argued that the decline began in the 1960s when the mass parties that had performed the classic articulation/aggregation/mediation function began to be challenged by new 'catch-all' people's parties: 'a more competitive model that tried to undo the old emphasis on strong representational links, seeking to exchange "effectiveness in depth for a wider audience and more immediate electoral success"' (2013: 82). Since then, the political parties had all but ceased to fulfil their representative role, becoming focused on their governing role: the recruitment of political leaders and the staffing of public offices, and the organisation of parliament and Government.[11] In the process they became ever more distanced from the people whose interests they formerly represented (or at least claimed to represent).

William Davies (2020) argues that liberal democracy (party politics, the public sphere of newspapers and broadcasters) is being weakened by the combination of Neoliberalism and digitisation. Neoliberalism has dissolved the boundaries between economics and politics. In an age of limitless bandwidth and ubiquitous data capture, digitisation has undermined organisations like political parties that seek to mediate between individual voters and the whole community:

> *The overarching theme is for a shift from a liberal polity based around norms, laws, expertise and institutions to a neoliberal one based around algorithmic surveillance and financial calculation.* (Davies, 2020: 24)

Davies sees populism as 'really a longing for some version of the [protective] state that predated neoliberal reforms' (2020: 16).

In fact, populism and technocracy may be seen as symptoms of the decline of party democracy. But is this the whole story?

6.7   Democracy in America

There can be little doubt that one of the chief reasons for the growth of populism in the US has been the perceived unresponsiveness of the political system to the concerns of many ordinary people. This in turn reflects the way in which a concentration of political power is coming to parallel the concentration of economic power that has accompanied increased inequality: what Robert Putnam, in a particularly felicitous phrase, describes (2020: 4) as 'a dangerous mutuality between wealth and power' (this was of course the central theme of the work by Hacker and Pierson summarised in Chap. 5).

A number of studies have shown how US politicians only take serious account of the views and interests of wealthy individuals, organised interest groups mostly oriented towards business, and big business.

In a 2009 article, Jeffrey A. Winters and Benjamin I. Page used data on US distributions of income and wealth to construct several Material Power Indices. These suggested that only a tiny proportion of the population—perhaps the top tenth of 1%—has sufficient power to dominate policy in key areas such as international economic policy, monetary policy, tax policy and, more broadly, any areas where redistribution may be an issue. This is accomplished through lobbying, funding elections and opinion shaping, as well as through the protection afforded for private property and wealth under the US Constitution. The Trump tax cuts are a classic instance of the power of this lobby, as is continued deregulation.[12]

In a 2014 study, Gilens and Page used a multivariate analysis of a unique data set, including the key variables for 1779 policy issues, to show that economic elites and organised business groups have substantial independent impacts on US Government policy while average citizens and mass-based interest groups have little or no such independent influence. A more recent analysis by McGuire and Delahunt (2020) uses a different statistical technique but confirms the dominance of corporations and the very wealthy in determining policy outcomes across a wide range of areas. Separate analyses by Ferguson and colleagues (1995, 2013, 2019, 2020) show how money flows are excellent predictors of the outcomes of congressional elections—'follow the money' indeed. Finally, a 2020 book by Page and Gilens brings all this together and shows exactly how wealthy groups manage to control US politics.[13]

Unfortunately, the calculated neglect of ordinary voters is not confined to the US although published studies elsewhere are rare. However, Will Jennings has pointed me to two European studies.

Giger et al. (2012) documented a general trend of under-representation of the preferences of poor citizens by both parties and governments across the Western democracies although they found important cross-national differences. Looking at 25 European countries between 2002 and 2010, Peters and Ensink (2015) found clear differences in responsiveness between higher- and lower-income groups: when the different groups' preferences do not align, governments tend to follow the preferences of the rich. The authors think that one of the reasons may be levels of voter turnout: especially low levels of turnout seem to emphasise over-representation of the rich and under-representation of the poor. This no doubt explains the vigorous efforts of the Republicans to minimise voting in poorer and minority areas in the US: 'voter suppression' (see Chap. 7). I have not been able to find any comparable UK studies but the fact that the Vote Leave campaign was largely funded by overseas-based oligarchs (Monbiot, 2020) should surely give us pause (possible changes to party financing are considered in Chap. 7).

6.8   Political Inequality

Robert Kuttner (2018) comments on the growth of 'political inequality'. As America has become less equal, the 'art of associating together' celebrated by Alexis De Tocqueville (1840) has been in steep decline:

> *Civic and political association and the organised exercise of influence have all but collapsed for the bottom half, dwindled for the bottom three-quarters, and intensified for the elite* (Kuttner, 2018: 17).

Kuttner suggests three trends—beyond growing income and wealth gaps and in the context of a mass society—that have exacerbated this decline:

> *Large mass-membership organizations that once engaged lower- and middle-class Americans in civic and political life have atrophied. Second, an entire habitat of mutual self-help organizations, ranging from unions to local buildings and loan societies, which also served as a civic training ground and an avenue of influence for the non-rich, have been substantially depleted as well.*

Finally, the mass entry of women into the labor force without a proportional reduction in the hours worked by most men has deprived localities of civic capital. (Kuttner, 2018: 19)

We shall return to the role of intermediate organisations in Chap. 7.

6.9   Political Marketing

Finally, we should note Robert Busby's interesting theory (2009) that what we are now seeing is a new form of 'political marketing' where— alongside the conventional criteria about policies and fitness for office— political understanding is now founded upon perceptions of who a candidate is, how they are perceived socially and how their emotional understanding impacts on the electorate. Of prime consideration is the presentation of the candidate as a person who is similar to, and shares the experiences of, the electorate (Busby, 2009: 199).

Alongside this there is a superficial aspect to the presentation, as a crossover into celebrity culture threatens to reduce politics (and the practice of democracy in particular) to a personality contest where policy discussion and understanding are secondary features for important elements within the voting block. This new political marketing enables the voter to make associations on grounds that require little in the way of political knowledge and to base evaluations on attributes to which they can relate.

Busby explains such marketing in terms of the need to capture the attention of voters in the middle ground when the parties' competing offers are very similar.[14]

6.10   The Sources of Authoritarian
Populism: Discussion

There is a high degree of commonalty in the forces that are thought to be driving or contributing to AP: globalisation, skill-biased-technological-change, financialisation and de-unionisation, all initiated or facilitated by Neoliberal policies of privatisation, deregulation and deflation/austerity. Together with market compression and corporate welfare, these have restructured many areas of the economy into 'winner-take-all' markets with increasingly sharp divisions between a small number of 'winners' and growing numbers of 'losers' (Frank & Cook, 2010). There is also broad agreement that these developments are rendering our customary

Right-Left political cleavages and affiliations obsolete.[15] But there is less consensus on how we might undo AP (always assuming this to be desirable).

Because they see AP as essentially a cultural phenomenon, Norris and Inglehart think it will disappear when (but only when) its supporters pass (if not sooner, if only younger and better educated people can be enabled and/or encouraged to vote). Similarly, Sobolewska and Ford (2020) see the conservatives' ability to exploit cultural wars as a wasting asset: continued educational expansion and demographic trends will mean that 'identity liberals' will soon outnumber 'identity conservatives'. This indeed was acknowledged by a leading Republican Senator in 2016:

> *The demographics race we're losing badly. We're not generating enough angry white guys to stay in business for the long term.* (Senator Lindsay Graham speaking at the 2016 Republican Convention, quoted in Younge, 2020)

Similarly, President Trump said on *Fox and Friends* in March 2020 that Democrats want 'levels of voting that, if ever you agreed to it, you'd never have a Republican elected in this country again' (Quoted in O'Toole, 2020).

In contrast, the contributors to the edited volume on the squeezed middle (Parker, 2013) argue for a more active policy stance: raising the minimum wage to a true living wage, increasing worker security through the strengthening of unions and other labour market intermediaries, increased investment in child- and eldercare, greater employer flexibility, and improving intermediate households' engagement and effectiveness in politics.

There is a good deal of overlap here with Azmanova's (2019) proposals. She envisages creating a 'political economy of trust': a political economy that supplies secure sources of livelihood while allowing everyone to profit from the increased decommodification capacity of advanced modernity. There are two main elements.

First, reforming globalisation by using non-tariff barriers to enshrine in international law high standards of employment and remuneration, consumer protection and care for the environment. Second, recasting domestic policy by (a) making labour market entry and exit easier, and (b) detaching social security from labour market participation: de-liberalising labour markets (in the Netherlands part-time employment is highly regulated). The aim is to minimise reliance on paid employment for both an individual's socialisation and the satisfaction of needs. This can be paid for by taxing the rich and socialising the rents from firms not exposed to competition (if not actually nationalising them).

There is some commonalty here with Michael Sandel's programme for rebuilding society along less meritocratic lines. Sandel proposes that the importance of higher education as a sorting mechanism should be reduced by introducing a greater degree of randomness in university admissions (beyond a threshold test) and shifting resources and priorities to lower level, post-school education that still serves the majority. The labour market should be transformed by active labour market policies that help workers to find the jobs, qualifications and skills they need.[16] Above all, we must switch our focus away from consumption to production and 'give all work activities a shape that reveals them to be a contribution to the common good' (p.211). This means clarifying what kinds of work are worthy of recognition and esteem (nurses rather than hedge fund managers), and what we owe one another as citizens (Sandel, 2020: 221).

6.11   Conclusion

This chapter reviewed theories for the resurgence of authoritarian populism. It distinguished cultural and economic explanations. The Brexit vote and the 2016 support for Donald Trump were seen as instances of a series of developments—especially rising inequality, economic insecurity and digitisation—that may together be undermining liberal democracy and parliamentary parties. Beyond reducing inequality and restoring economic growth, this review suggests that the starting point for reversing AP should be reforms to make the political system more responsive to the electorate as a whole and less sensitive to capital, as well as more inclusive. These are themes that we shall pursue in Chap. 7.

Notes

1. The term 'fictional' refers to Benedict Anderson's classic (2006) argument that 'nations' are essentially cultural constructs.
2. We noted in Chap. 5 Robert Kuttner's (2018) comments about the extent to which, once in power, Trump jettisoned most of his anti-elite policies. In December 2016 the combined wealth of his initial Cabinet was estimated as $13bn (Rocheleau, 2016).
3. However, we shall note in Chap. 7 evidence that the Covid crisis may be leading to some cooling of support for populist parties and leaders.

4. Bill Bishop (2009) argues that increased physical mobility since the 1960s is enabling more of us to live in like-minded clusters, and that this in turn is contributing to increased polarisation simply because we have little regular contact with those who may disagree with us.

5. For a similar view, see Economist (2016). Reporting on a survey of Leavers' and Remainers' attitudes conducted by UK in a Changing Europe and the independent social research agency NatCen, Simon Kuper (2020b) found that Leavers' chief bogey wasn't the EU or Remainers but benefits scroungers, not only immigrants but home-grown ones as well.

6. However, an unpublished 2020 paper by Adam Wheeler and the author analysing current ONS data on multiple deprivation cautions against simply equating deprivation with any one part of the country. Contrary to what is often supposed, deprivation can be found across all regions, and it is just more visible in the North. So 'levelling-up' shouldn't be confined to the Red Wall areas, but requires a well thought through, targeted approach to deprivation across the whole country. A 2020 analysis by Calvert Jump and Mitchell also cautions against a simple equation of deprivation with Leave.

7. It is incidentally hard to see how Covid will help here, let alone Brexit. Virtually every independent study has found that in view of the likely effect on public revenues and welfare spending, middle- and low-income households are likely to bear a disproportionate share of the costs of Brexit (e.g., Hantzsche and Young 2019; McGrade, 2020). Similarly, poorer areas have been more heavily hit by Covid than wealthier ones: Barr and Halliday (2020), Boseley (2020), Covid Recovery Commission (2020), Blundell et al. (2022), Gregory (2022). In many cases this is because they have a long history of poor housing and health conditions. They also have low rates of vaccination (as in the US, where there is a strong correlation between counties that voted for Trump and those with the highest levels of infection: Charter 2021).

8. Bernard Abramson (personal communication) comments that in their resentment, desperation and anger, such groups will vote for anyone who promises—possibly in code, and even quite unbelievably—to return matters to the earlier state. The promisers are usually conservative, right-wing parties. What happens when the return to the status quo ante inevitably fails to be realised? Trump's policies have not reversed the economic decline of the Rust Belt, Johnson's policies will almost certainly fail to 'level up' the 'left behind' areas. If anything, the AP's supporters then become even more fervent (underlining the value of loyalty). They can't admit that they were wrong and are in part the authors of their own misery. But by this time many of the democratic norms and institutions that might

have enabled a more balanced solution to their problems may have been destroyed.

9. Studying the evolution of American regional cultures, David Hallett Fischer (1989) argued that the origins of slavery in the US were as much cultural and social as economic:

> *In an effort to preserve a cultural hegemony ... the gentry of Virginia would develop a novel type of race slavery on a large scale – a radical innovation with profound consequences for the future ... these new forms of slavery did not create the culture of the tidewater Virginia; that culture created slavery.* (Fischer, 1989: 255–6)

Fischer showed how many of the early Virginian families came from parts of England (broadly, Wessex) that had had serfs in earlier times. Moreover, the social composition of Virginia was unusual because a high proportion of settlers came as indentured servants and wanted/needed someone to look down on. In a December 2021 review of Edward Ball's *Life of a Klansman: A Personal History of White Supremacy* (Farrar et al., 2021), Colin Grant quotes (a typically cynical) Lyndon Johnson as saying in the late-1960s, 'If you can convince the lowest white man he's better than the best colored man, he won't notice you're picking his pocket. Hell, give him somebody to look down on, and he'll empty his pockets for you'.

10. The present Secretary of State for Levelling Up, Housing and Communities, Michael Gove became famous for his comment, during a Sky News interview at the height of the Brexit campaign in which he declined to name any Brexit-backing economists, that 'people in this country have had enough of experts' (Mance, 2016). In Tim Shipman's (jaw-dropping) account of the Brexit campaigns, the author quotes Ryan Coetzee, Stronger Leave's Head of Strategy, as to what lay behind this comment:

> *More than any specific ideological vision he has, Gove is an ideologue. You do get the whiff of burning witches. The thing about ideologues ... none of them need experts because they're the expert; because the ideology has the answer. Ideologues force the world to conform to their theory instead of having their theory conform to the world. That, to my mind, explains Michael Gove.* (Shipman, 2016: 326, original author's emphases)

11. It is therefore interesting that even the wealthy Donald Trump felt the need for Republican nomination for his election bids.

12. For the Trump tax cuts, see Chap. 5, Note 12. The regulatory picture may be changing with President Biden's recent appointment of the strongly pro-regulatory Lina Khan to the key post of head of the Federal Trade Commission (Foroohar, 2022).

13. Clearly, the main means is through money, not only in financing election campaigns but also between them. The elite have been helped by court judgements that have progressively narrowed the definition of corruption and stripped away the limits on private funding. The money power also explains why, whatever their own views, so many candidates have to toe the party line. The bulk of political representatives and officials are also drawn from the ranks of the wealthy (according to Open Secrets, a majority of members of the current Congress are millionaires—Evers-Hillstrom, 2020). At the same time, the very wealthy are reticent about making their views public. This is why accounts of their behind-the-scenes funding and lobbying activities, such as Mayer, J. (2016) and MacLean (2017), are so valuable. The 'radical rich' (Frum, 2014) have also been helped by the parallel decline of many mass membership organisations, notably the trade unions, in part because of Neoliberal policies. We shall look at conservative efforts to take control of the courts in Chap. 7.

14. This approach is well reflected in the reported remark of Boris Johnson during a crisis in his time as London Mayor:

    Don't worry. The show – and it is a show – will go on. (Shipman, 2022)

    William Davies (2019) has coined the term 'Berlusconification' to describe this process.

15. For instance, Thomas Piketty (2018) has suggested a new cleavage between a 'Brahmin left' (high-education, high-income) and a 'Merchant right' (low-education, low-income).

16. Recent research under the aegis of the Institute of Labour Economics (Bertheau et al., 2022) shows how effective Active Labour Management Programmes can be in moderating earnings losses after job displacement. (I owe this reference to Nye Cominetti at the Resolution Foundation.)

REFERENCES

Anderson, B. (2006). *Imagined communities* (Revised ed.), Verso.
Antonucci, L., Horvath, L., Kutiyski, Y., & Krouwel, A. (2017). The malaise of the squeezed middle: Challenging the narrative of the "left behind" Brexiter. *Competition and Change, 21*(3), 211–229.
Arbair, P. (2016, November 23). Brexit, the populist surge and the crisis of complexity. *Paul Arbair*. Retrieved November 24, 2016, from https://paularbair. wordpress.com/2016/07/05/Brexit-the-populist-surge-and-the-crisis-of-complexity/
Azmanova, A. (2019). *Capitalism on edge.* Columbia University Press.
Ball, E. (2021). *Life of a Klansman: A family history of white supremacy.* Farrar, Straus and Giroux.

Barr, C., & Halliday, J. (2020, October 8). Poorest areas of England four times as likely to face lockdown as richest. *The Guardian*.

Behr, R. (2020, August 26). He was a tonic for the Tories. Now Johnson is turning toxic. *The Guardian Opinion*.

Bell, T. (2016, June 24). *The referendum, living standards and inequality*. Retrieved June 28, 2016, from www.resolutionfoundation.org/media/blogs/the-referendum-living-standards-and-inequality/.

Bell, B., & Machin, S. (2016, August 16). *Brexit and wage inequality*. VoxEU.org. Retrieved August 27, 2020, from https://voxeu.org/article/brexit-and-wage-inequality

Bertheau, A., Acabbi, E., Barcelo, C., Gulyas, A., Lombardi, S., & Saggio, R. (2022). *The unequal cost of job loss across countries*. IZA Institute of Labor Economics Discussion Paper No. 15033.

Bickerton, C., & Invenizzi Accetti, C. (2015). Populism and technocracy: Opposites or complements? *Critical Review of International Social and Political Philosophy*, 20(2), 186–206. https://doi.org/10.1080/1369823 0.2014.995504

Blundell, R., Costa Dias, M., Cribb, J., Joyce, R., Waters, T., Wernham, T., & Xu, X. (2022). *Inequality and the Covid crisis in the United Kingdom*. Institute for Fiscal Studies Working Paper 22/01. Institute for Fiscal Studies.

Boseley, S. (2020, October 27). 'Perfect storm': 30 years of failure on preventable diseases fuels pandemic. *The Guardian*.

British Election Study. (2016, October 6). *Brexit Britain: British election study insights from the post-EU Referendum wave of the BES internet panel*. http://www.britishelectionstudy.com/bes-resources/brexit-britain-british-election-study-insights-from-the-post-eu-referendum-wave-of-the-bes-internet-panel/.

Bukodi, E., & Goldthorpe, J. H. (2021). *Meritocracy and populism: Is there a connection?* UK in a Changing Europe (UKICE) Working Paper 01/2021.

Burn-Murdoch, J. (2017, October 18). The six tribes of Brexit revealed. *Financial Times*. Retrieved October 19, 2017, from https://www.ft.com/content/61c12868-b350-11e7-a398-73d59db9e399.

Busby, R. (2009). *Marketing the populist politician: The demotic democrat*. Palgrave Macmillan.

Centre for Social Investigation. (2020). *Briefing Paper CSI21: Social class mobility in modern Britain: changing structure, constant process*. University of Oxford Centre for Social Investigation.

Clarke, S. (2016, October 12). *Brexit means…different things to different people*. Resolution Foundation. Retrieved October 16, 2016, from https://www.resolutionfoundation.org/comment/Brexit-means-different-things-to-different-people/.

Clinton, J. (2022, January 17). Will the BBC licence fee be scrapped? 17 January. *i News*. Retrieved February 1, 2022, from https://inews.co.uk/culture/

television/bbc-licence-fee-scrapped-will-nadine-dorries-when-abolished-replacement-1405227.

Covid Recovery Commission. (2020). *Levelling up communities*. Retrieved October 16, 2020, from www.covidrecoverycommission.co.uk/wp-content/uploads/2020/10/Levelling-up-communities.pdf.

Cultural Dynamics. (2016). *Can the UK expect to have less Prospectors in the near future as a result of the Brexit vote?* Retrieved October 21, 2016, from http://www.cultdyn.co.uk/ART067736u/ProspPost Brex.html.

Curtice, J. (2016). *How deeply does Britain's Euroscepticism run?* Retrieved January 24, 2022, from https://www.bsa.natcen.ac.uk/media/39024/euroscepticism.pdf.

Dalio, F., Kryger, S., Rogers, J., & Davis, G. (2017, March 22). Populism: The phenomenon. *Bridgepoint Daily Observations*. Retrieved January 19, 2018, from https://www.bridgewater.com/resources/bwam032217.pdf.

Davies, W. (2019, December 4). *How Boris Johnson and Brexit are Berlusconifying Britain*. Retrieved January 4, 2022, from https://www.theguardian.com/commentisfree/2019/dec/04/boris-johnson-brexit-britain-politics-media-business.

Davies, W. (2020). *This is not normal: The collapse of liberal Britain*. Verso.

De Tocqueville, A. (1840). *Democracy in America* (repr. New York: Vintage 1945).

Dorling, D. (2018). *Peak inequality: Britain's ticking time bomb*. Policy Press.

Economist. (2016, July 30). *Drawbridges up*. https://www.economist.com/briefing/2016/07/30/drawbridges-up.

Eichengreen, B. (2018). *The populist temptation: Economic grievance and political reaction in the modern Era*. Oxford University Press.

Engels, F. (1893, July 14). *Letter to Franz Mehring*. International Publishers. Retrieved October 6, 2018, from https://www.marxists.org/archive/marx/works/1893/letters/93_07_14.htm.

Evers-Hillstrom, K. (2020, April 23). Majority of lawmakers in 116th Congress are millionaires. *Open Secrets*. Retrieved May 25, 2021, from https://www.opensecrets.org/news/2020/04/majority-of-lawmakers-millionaires/.

Ferguson, T. (1995). *Golden rule: The investment theory of party competition and the logic of money-driven political systems*. Chicago University Press.

Ferguson, T. (2013). Review of *Affluence and Influence: Economic inequality and political power in America* by Martin Gilens. *Princeton University Press. Perspectives on Politics, 11*(1), 252–254.

Ferguson, T., Jorgensen, P., & Chen, J. (2019, September). How money drives US congressional elections: Linear models of money and outcomes. *Structural Change and Economic Dynamics*. https://doi.org/10.1016/j.strueco.2019.09.005

Ferguson, T., Jorgensen, P., & Chen, J. (2020). *How much can the U.S. congress resist political money? A quantitative assessment.* Institute for New Economic Thinking Working Paper No. 109.

Fetzer, T., Sasche, O. B., & Novy, D. (2018). *Austerity, immigration or globalisation: Was Brexit predictable?* Social Market Foundation and Competitive Advantage in the Global Economy.

Finch, D. (2016). *Hanging on. The stresses and strains of Britain's just managing families.* Resolution Foundation.

Fischer, D. H. (1989). *Albion's seed: Four British folkways in America.* Oxford University Press.

Foroohar, R. (2022, January 17). What Biden's competition crusade tells us about globalisation. *Financial Times.* Retrieved January 17, 2022, from https://www.ft.com/content/e0692dca-cdd7-4ae1-87d7-e8310d501ef8.

Frank, T. (2004). *What's the matter with Kansas? How Conservatives won the heart of America.* Picador.

Frank, R. H., & Cook, P. J. (2010). *The winner-take-all-society: Why the few at the top get so much more.* Virgin.

Frum, D. (2014, January 9). *Crashing the party.* Retrieved January 9, 2021, from https://davidfrum.com/article/crashing-the-party.

Giger, N., Rosset, J., & Bernauer, J. (2012). The poor political representation of the poor in a comparative perspective. *Journal of Representative Democracy, 48,* 47–61.

Goodhart, D. (2020). *Head, hand, heart: The struggle for dignity and status in the 21st Century.* Penguin.

Goodwin, M., & Heath, O. (2016, July 26). *Brexit and the left behind: A tale of two countries.* Retrieved July 26, 2016, from. http://blogs.lse.ac.uk/brexitvote/2016/07/22/brexit-and-the-left-behind-a-tale-of-two-countries.

Grant, C. (2021). Sins of the Fathers. Review of *Life of a Klansman: A family history of white supremacy.* Farrar, Straus and Giroux. *New York Review of Books* 18 November, pp. 4–7.

Gray, A. (2021, December 14). UK government vetoes reappointment of another two Channel 4 directors. *Financial Times.* Retrieved December 15, 2022, from https://www.ft.com/content/9be74f15-8ba7-45a9-9cc7-98ae7960a204.

Gregory, A. (2022, February 16) Covid-19 impact deadlier for poor areas than first thought. *The Guardian.*

Hacker, J. S., & Pierson, P. (2020). *Let Them eat tweets: How the right rules in an age of extreme inequality.* Liveright.

Haidt, J. (2013). *The righteous mind: Why people are divided by politics and religion.* Penguin.

Hantzsche, A., & Young, G. (2019, November). *UK general election briefing: The economic and fiscal impact of Brexit.* National Institute of Economic and Social Research and Nuffield Foundation.

Holmwood, J. (2014). Beyond capital? The challenge for sociology in Britain. *The British Journal of Sociology, 65*(4), 607–618.

Jennings, W. (2016, June 3). North v South, young v old – the new faultlines of UK's political map. *The Observer.*

Jennings, W. (2020, November 8). Educated urban voters were key to success in deeply divided electorate. *The Observer.*

Joseph Rowntree Foundation. (2016). *Brexit vote explained: poverty, low skills and lack of opportunities.*https://www.jrf.org.uk/report/brexit-vote-explained-poverty-low-skills-and-lack-opportunities.

Konczal, M. (2021). *Freedom from the market: America's fight to liberate itself from the grip of the invisible hand.* The New Press.

Kuper, S. (2020a, February 15–16). The revenge of the middle-class anti-elitist. *Financial Times Magazine.*

Kuper, S. (2020b, October 17–18). What Leavers and Remainers really think now. *Financial Times Magazine.*

Kuttner, R. (2018). *Can democracy survive global capitalism?* W.W.Norton.

Luce, E. (2017). *The retreat of western liberalism.* Abacus.

MacLean, N. (2017). *Democracy in chains: The deep history of the radical right's stealth plan for America.* Scribe.

Mair, P. (2013). *Ruling the void: The hollowing of western democracy.* Verso.

Malik, N. (2020, August 31). The right's culture war is no sideshow. It's our politics now. *The Guardian Opinion.*

Mance, H. (2016, June 3). Britain has had enough of experts, says Gove. *Financial Times.*

Mayer, J. (2016). *Dark money: The hidden history of the billionaires behind the rise of the radical right.* Scribe.

McCurdy, C., Gardiner, L., Gustafsson, M., & Handscomb, K. (2020). *Painting the towns blue: Demography, economy and living standards in the political geographies emerging from the 2019 General Election.* Resolution Foundation.

McGrade, P. (2020). *Manufacturing in the marginals.* Retrieved October 22, 2020, from https://lexreports.readz.com/manufacturing-report-final-for-web.pdf.

McGuire, S. K., & Delahunt, C. B. (2020). *Predicting United States policy outcomes with random forests.* Institute for New Economic Thinking Working Paper 138.

Monbiot, G. (2020, November 25). There is a civil war in capitalism and we're the collateral damage. *The Guardian Journal.*

Mudde, C. (2015, February 17). The problem with populism. *The Guardian.* Retrieved November 8, 2021, from https://www.theguardian.com/commentisfree/2015/feb/17/problem-populism-syriza-podemos-dark-side-europe.

Mueller, J.-W. (2016). *What is populism?* University of Pennsylvania Press.

Mueller, J.-W. (2021a). *Democracy rules.* Allen Lane.

Mueller, J.-W. (2021b, December 9). Biden is selling democracy short. *The New York Times*. Retrieved December 9, 2021, from https://www.nytimes.com/2021/12/09/opinion/biden-democracy-summit.html.

Niven, A. (2020, September 20). England's new divide: not north v south but town v city. *The Guardian Journal*.

Norris, P., & Inglehart, R. (2019). *Cultural backlash: Trump, Brexit and authoritarian populism*. Cambridge University Press.

O'Toole, F. (2020, December 3). Democracy's afterlife. *The New York Review of Books*.

Parker, S. (Ed.). (2013). *The squeezed middle: The pressure on ordinary workers in America and Britain*. Policy Press.

Payne, S. (2021). *Broken heartlands: A journey through Labour's lost England*. Macmillan.

Peters, Y., & Ensink, S. J. (2015). Differential responsiveness in Europe: The effects of preference difference and electoral participation. *West European Politics, 38*(3), 577–600. https://doi.org/10.1080/01402382.2014.973260

Piketty, T. (2018). *Brahmin Left vs Merchant Right: Rising inequality and the changing structure of political conflict (Evidence from France, Britain and the US, 1948–2017)*. Retrieved August 28, 2020, from http://piketty.pse.ens.fr/files/Piketty2018.pdf.

Pissarides, C., Skordi, J., Tomas, A., Atwell, S., & De Lyons, J. (2019). *Automation, politics and the future of work: A discussion paper*. Institute for the Future of Work. https://static1.squarespace.com/static/5aa269bbd274cb0df1e696c8/t/5de4d89235fa141ad0cd1679/1575278743066/Automation%2C+politics+and+the+future+of+work+.pdf.

Rocheleau, M. (2016, December 20). Trump's Cabinet picks so far worth a combined $13b. *The Boston Globe*. Retrieved February 15, 2022, from https://www.bostonglobe.com/metro/2016/12/20/trump-cabint-picks-far-are-worth-combined/XvAJmHCgkHhO31SxgIKvRM/story.html.

Rosenbaum, M. (2017, February 6). *Local voting figures shed new light on EU referendum*. http://www.bbc.co.uk/news/uk-politics-38762034.

Ruggie, J. (1982). International regimes, transactions, and change: Embedded Liberalism in the postwar economic order. *International Organization, 36*, 379–415.

Runciman, D. (2019). *How democracy ends*. Profile.

Sandel, M. J. (2020). *The tyranny of merit: What's become of the common good?* Allen Lane.

Shipman, T. (2016). *All out war: The full story of how Brexit Sank Britain's political class*. William Collins.

Shipman, T. (2022, January 2). A sticky situation. *The Sunday Times*

Sobolewska, M., & Ford, R. (2020). *Brexitland: Identity, diversity and the reshaping of British politics*. Cambridge University Press.

Stoller, M. (2016, October 24). How democrats killed their populist soul. *The Atlantic*. Retrieved November 12, 2016, from http://www.theatlantic.com/politics/archive/2016/10/how-democrats-killed-their-populist-soul/504710/.

Techau, P. (2016 April 19). Sophisticated states are failing – politicians need to take risks. *Financial Times*. Retrieved August 27, 2020, from https://www.ft.com/content/f519492e-022b-11e6-99cb-83242733f755.

Vance, J. D. (2016). *Hillbilly elegy: A memoir of a family and culture in crisis*. Harper Collins.

Walker, P. (2018, October 27). Divided Britain: Polling study finds huge chasm in attitudes. *The Guardian*.

Westlake, S. (2016, July 1). *U can't touch this: Why the intangible economy makes people vote for Brexit*. Retrieved January 18, 2019, from http://www.theintangibleeconomy.com/?p=83.

Wilkerson, I. (2020). *Caste: The origins of our discontents*. Random House.

Wright, O. (2019, February 4). Experts blame Brexit on coalition austerity. *The Times*.

Younge, G. (2020, November 17). The unfinished business of American democracy. *The Guardian Long Read*.

CHAPTER 7

The Conservative Counter-revolution

Abstract The main part of this chapter analyses the ways in which the major conservative parties on both sides of the Atlantic have successfully reversed many of the policies associated with the New Deal and the welfare state and the long period of Keynesianism after 1945. These ways include a willingness to break longstanding legal and constitutional arrangements, to destroy or marginalise alternative centres of power, to exploit the economic crises that are the inevitable concomitant of free market capitalism, and to capitalise on deep social and cultural grievances. The conservatives have been assisted in this by the readiness of some progressive parties to accept and even endorse Neoliberalism, and to switch their focus from economic to social and cultural issues. In the final part, we make some suggestions about how the progressive parties might go about staging a 'progressive counter-counter-revolution'.

Keywords Conservative Party • Conservatism • Neoliberalism • Republican Party

This is the essence of the Conservative Party's role—to formulate policy that conserves a hierarchy of wealth and power, and to make this intelligible and reasonable to a democracy. (Norton & Aughey, *1981*: 47)

© The Author(s), under exclusive license to Springer Nature 115
Switzerland AG 2022
R. Brown, *The Conservative Counter-Revolution in Britain and America 1980–2020*,
https://doi.org/10.1007/978-3-031-09142-1_7

> *The persistent trick of modern politics ... one that appears to fool us repeatedly ... is to disguise economic and political interests as cultural movements.* (Monbiot, 2020)

It is hard to disagree with those writers (e.g., Frank, 2004; Dionne, 2016, Hacker and Pierson seriatim) who have argued that what we have seen in the US since the late 1970s has been a conservative revolt against the New Deal and the Civil Rights movement and the associated expansion of state activity and minority rights. This rightward shift has turned into a bitterly anti-progressive crusade for low taxes, minimal Government and only the most basic levels of social protection. As many relatively moderate Republicans have found, it takes no hostages, whatever their political affiliation or the effect on governance. The success of this movement can be seen in the way in which the whole political centre of gravity has moved to the right, as confirmed by international surveys (e.g., Chinoy, 2019). A parallel process has taken place in Britain in reaction to the welfare state and the liberal social reforms of the 1960s and 1970s.[1]

In both countries, the principal beneficiaries have been the very wealthy, major companies and the financial sector. At the same time, inequality and poverty have increased, instability and precarity have risen, social mobility has gone into reverse, social cohesion and trust have been weakened, economic growth has fallen, and support for the political system has diminished. There has also been an external cost in the weakening of both countries' international reputations and influence. Nevertheless, since the late-1970s we have been governed either by parties of the Right (moving steadily rightwards) or by centre-left parties that have accepted the basic tenets of Neoliberalism and also moved rightwards.[2]

Why and how this has happened, given the enormous damage both countries have sustained as a result of these policies? Bluntly, how have the conservatives got away with it?

It may first be worth noting that the conservative parties' success in determining overall policy has not been reflected in vote shares at national elections. The share of the popular vote taken by Republican presidential candidates has fallen steadily from 61% (Richard Nixon's re-election in 1972) to 59% (Ronald Reagan), 51% (George W. Bush) and now 47% (Trump in 2020). George W. Bush was in fact the only Grand Old Party (G.O.P) candidate in the last 30 years to win the popular vote. Moreover, even in the closest election of the last half-century (2000) the national popular vote margin was still more than half a million (Epstein & Corasaniti, 2022a). In Britain since the War, the conservatives' share of the general election vote has always been smaller than that of the other, mostly progressive, parties (House of Commons Library, 2020).

Nor has the conservative parties' dominance been due to executive effectiveness. Of the Conservative Party's three most recent leaders (to mid-July 2022), one had to resign after leaving the EU against his intention, one was defeated by having to sort out the ensuing mess, and the leadership of the last made his Government a synonym for incompetence and mistrust. In the US, President Trump's administration quickly became a byword for cronyism, incoherence and inefficiency.

Even more strikingly, both major conservative parties have increasingly been driven by a minority of extremist activists only partially representative of conservative opinion at large, let alone the general population—Newt Gingrich and the Tea Party, Nigel Farage and UKIP, the European Research Group, the Net Zero Scrutiny Group—but whom the mainstream leadership has preferred to appease, rather than confront. The extremists have been assisted by the skew in governance—starting with first-past-the-post and single-member constituencies—that reduces the incentive to appeal to voters outside the party's core base, and which is one of the cornerstones of the adversarial politics that we encountered in Chap. 3.

Let us now return to the question of 'why and how'. The starting point is the appreciation that, ironically, 'conservatism' is not necessarily conservative at all.

In *The Reactionary Mind: Conservatism from Edmund Burke to Donald Trump* (2018), the American political scientist Corey Robin argues that conservatism is essentially a reactionary code, and one that can be either conservative in the ordinary sense of the word (i.e., preservative) or radical (and even counter-revolutionary) where it seeks to resist the broadening of power away from elites or dominant groups, or to restore power to those groups:

> *Typically, the conservative attempts to conserve, to hold on to the values of the existing society...But...what if the existing society is inherently hostile to conservative beliefs? It is foolish for a conservative to attempt to conserve that culture. Rather, he must seek to undermine it, to thwart it, to destroy it at the root level. This means that the conservative must be philosophically conservative but temperamentally radical.* (Robin, 2018: 26)

Consistent with this thesis, both the US Republicans and the British Conservatives have been quite prepared to tweak, or even break, the rules of governance (whilst portraying themselves, ironically, as the parties of 'law and order'). Both have been prepared to attack, discredit and undermine governing institutions, and to depict Government (and the wider public sector) as weak, inefficient and even corrupt. At the same time, they have sought to avoid direct scrutiny or accountability for their actions wherever possible.

In the US, the most serious example to date was President Trump's refusal, along with a majority of Republican party members (see below), to accept the outcome of the 2020 election. David Runciman (2019: 14) describes as 'the minimal definition of democracy ... that the losers of an election accept that they have lost' (cf. Wolf, 2021). In Britain, the most egregious case (so far) was Boris Johnson's advice to the Queen in August 2019 to prorogue parliament, a decision subsequently ruled unlawful by the Supreme Court. This judgement was in turn called 'a constitutional coup' by the Leader of the House of Commons, Jacob Rees-Mogg (Rutter, 2019).

The Government is now attempting through the Judicial Review and Courts Act 2022 to enable Ministers to overrule judicial review findings that challenge their decisions. The new Police, Crime, Scrutiny and Courts Actl contains additional restrictions on the right to protest. The new Bill of Rights Bill would enable Ministers to ignore injunctions from the European Court of Human Rights which was established after World War II by Winston Churchill and Sir David Maxwell-Fyfe. This follows the Court's ban on the Home Secretary putting asylum seekers on a plane to Rwanda. The Government is also seeking to limit parliamentary scrutiny of the post-Brexit trade agreements (Hayter, 2022). It is quite remarkable that the same 'libertarian' conservative MPs who have opposed the Government's anti-Covid restrictions have not seen any difficulty with these much more serious threats to democracy.

In the US, there has been substantial voter suppression.[3] However, this is now starting here as well. The Elections Act would require photo ID at future elections. According to the Government's own analysis, this could lead to more than two million people being disenfranchised, disproportionately older, poorer, disabled and homeless voters (Walker et al., 2021). As well as imposing additional restrictions on voting (especially by post), the US Republicans are giving Republican-controlled state legislatures greater control over the administration of elections so that the voters' will can be subverted if necessary (Corasaniti, 2022). They are also establishing new agencies to tackle voter fraud, even though there is very little evidence of this (Epstein & Corasaniti, 2022b). In the UK, the Government is seeking greater control over the Electoral Commission (which polices elections) after it fined the Conservative Party for failing to accurately report political donations (Cohen, 2021).

Paul Starr (2019) describes the various ways in which—typically—right-wing parties representing concentrated wealth bring about political changes that opponents find hard to reverse (Bernard Abramson, personal communication). Trump and the Republicans' haste to appoint a new Supreme Court judge (Amy Coney Barrett), so that the Court would have a strong conservative majority, even though the presidential election had already been called, is an excellent recent example.[4]

Gerrymandering is another strategy used by both US parties although mostly by the Republicans. Jamelle Bouie (2021a) identifies a number of key battleground states where Republicans are either creating 'supermajorities' capable of overriding a Governor's veto or whittling down competitive districts so that Republican advantage is almost impenetrable (leaving voters in narrowly divided states powerless to change the leadership of their legislatures).[5]

In both America and Britain, there has been strong mainstream media support from advocates/beneficiaries of these policies like Rupert Murdoch and Viscount Rothermere. This may be one of the reasons why both the Republicans and the conservatives have been so successful in 'shape shifting': adopting radically different policies without anyone much remarking on it. In the US, Republican attitudes to the public deficit seem to depend almost entirely on whether or not they are in power. In Britain, the difficulties facing the Labour Opposition stem partly from the fact that their signature policies of greater public spending and state intervention were adopted by Johnson's Conservatives (though not without serious internal dissension). It is even possible that in combining progressive economic policies (raising taxes to spend on health and infrastructure, bailing out failing energy companies) with a conservative cultural stance, the Conservatives may have a winning election hand.

At the same time, alternative centres of power have been reduced: the unions in both countries, in Britain local Government as well. Referring to the way in which comprehensive Neoliberal reforms were introduced in Chile, Nancy MacLean talks (2017: 156) of a 'state-induced fragmentation of group power'. Robert Kuttner (2018: 17) refers to William Kornhauser's *The Politics of Mass Society:*

Caesarism thrives when people are drawn to totalitarian dictators and "there is a paucity of intervening groups to channelize and filter popular participation in the larger society" (Kornhauser, 1959: 37).

This leads us inevitably to consider the relationship between conservatism, Neoliberalism and authoritarianism.

Reading MacLean's account of the Chilean reforms leaves little doubt that because it is so disrupting and damaging to most people, the application of the full Neoliberal programme can only be realised through sustained authoritarianism, as some of its protagonists have acknowledged.

Slobodian (2019) quotes Milton Friedman as saying, in a 1988 interview, 'I believe a relatively free economy is a necessary condition for freedom. But there is evidence that a democratic society, once established, destroys a free economy'. Monbiot (2020) reports Friedrich Hayek saying, on a visit to Pinochet's Chile, that he preferred 'a liberal dictatorship' to 'a democratic government devoid of liberalism'. Martin Wolf (2020) argues that just because it is so damaging to so many people, the only way libertarian economic ideas can win in a universal suffrage democracy is for them to be allied with ancillary causes: culture wars, racism, misogyny, nativism, xenophobia and nationalism, as we have seen with both Brexit and Trump and are now seeing with Johnson's English nationalist Government (Malik, N. 2020). It appears that—like war and peace—one can have either economic liberalism or political liberalism, but not both.

Moving on, both conservative parties have been quite ruthless in defending themselves, including (in the US) through the encouragement or condonement of violence: the Charlottesville rally in 2017 (which President Trump refused to condemn), armed attacks on a number of state capitols as well as on the Capitol (for the last of which President Trump almost certainly bears a considerable responsibility) and the growing mobilisation of far-right forces through unregulated social media (Chaffin, 2021; Clarke, 2021; Kanno-Youngs & Sanger, 2021; Rondeaux & Hurlburt, 2021). The Republican Party now even has a Congresswoman (Marjorie Taylor-Greene) who in 2019 endorsed the projected shooting of the House Speaker (Nancy Pelosi).[6]

In Britain, the murder of the Labour MP Jo Cox in June 2016 has not yet been followed, thankfully, by mass violence. But headlines such as 'Enemies of the People' in the *Daily Mail* in November 2016 (in response to the judges' decision that Brexit should be subject to a parliamentary vote, and with no attempt to defend the judiciary by Lord Chancellor

Truss in spite of her constitutional oath) have hardly been conducive to social harmony. The recent (December 2021) attacks on the Government's scientific and medical advisers (Sample, 2021) are par for this particular course.

Robin notes that conservatism has always been comfortable with violence. Referring to Edmund Burke, he writes:

> *Rule may be sublime, but violence is more sublime. Most sublime of all is where the two are fused, when violence is performed for the sake of creating, defending or recovering a regime of dominance or rule* (Robin, 2018: 61).

To be sure, America has a long history of mob violence, mostly aimed at blacks and other minorities (Sachs, 2021). Conservative parties in both countries have made covert, and sometimes overt, appeals to racism as a means of courting white working-class voters and making them think that they have that in common with their wealthier fellow citizens (Temin, 2017). Opposition to immigration is an aspect of this. This was of course a recurrent theme of the Trump Presidency. It is therefore unsurprising that recent research at the University of Massachusetts—Amherst (Edsall, 2022) finds striking linkages between attitudes on race and immigration, on the one hand, and disbelief in the integrity of the 2020 election, on the other.

In a very interesting 2017 paper, Charles L. Ballard argued that the increase in inequality in America was actually due to the way in which many whites, especially in the South, reacted to the Civil Rights movement by switching their allegiance to the Republicans:

> *White voters of modest economic circumstances supported the egalitarian policies that led to the Great Compression* [the reduction in inequality in the 30s and 40s associated with Keynesianism and the New Deal], *and this advanced their economic interests. Economic inequality was reduced dramatically, and the standard of living of low- and middle-income whites skyrocketed. However, when the federal government moved to reduce **racial** inequality, the support for egalitarian **economic** policies among low- and middle-income white voters was reduced enough to usher in the anti-egalitarian tide of the last 40 years, to the detriment of those same white voters.* (Ballard, 2017: 59, original author's emphases)

While overt racism has not been such a prominent feature of British politics, it is strongly arguable that the conservative fightback against welfare state liberalism began not with Mrs. Thatcher's election in 1979 but with Enoch Powell's 1968 'rivers of blood' speech. As Nick Cohen wrote in *The Observer* in 2020, 'Powell was a Thatcherite before Thatcherism, advocating privatisation and unashamed capitalism so vigorously that Friedrich Hayek (no less) said in 1965 "All our hopes in England now rest on Enoch Powell"' (Cohen, 2020). It seems an apt illustration of how far our politics has moved rightwards that whereas Powell was sacked from the Government Front Bench for his comments, the present Prime Minister has written of 'flag waving piccaninnies with watermelon smiles' (Bowcott & Jones, 2008).

This conservative reaction has extended to a sustained attack on the existing epistemic regime: the rules and understandings that govern the meaning and use of knowledge. A much quoted example was Trump Adviser's (Kellyanne Conway's) use of the term 'alternative facts' in January 2017 to describe the numbers attending Trump's Inauguration (Swaine, 2017). Many of Trump's supporters get all or most of their news information and comment from Murdoch's Fox News. Several commentators have actually argued that the damage to the common conception of reality (and the associated degree of trust) has been the most serious of the many and various ways in which Trump has damaged America. For example:

> ...it's hard to think of any person in my lifetime who so perfectly epitomizes the politics of distrust, or one who so aggressively promotes it. Trump has taught his opponents not to believe a word he says, his followers not to believe a word anyone else says, and much of the rest of the country to believe nobody and nothing at all.
>
> He has detonated a bomb under the epistomological foundations of a civilization that is increasingly unable to distinguish between facts and falsehoods, evidence and fantasy. He has instructed millions of people to accept the commandment, **That which you can get away with is true** (Stephens, B. 2020, original author's emphasis).

It is indeed very difficult to imagine anything that is more corrosive of a liberal democracy than an inability to agree on a shared basis of evidence and truth.

Frank Bruni (2021) argues that there is a direct line from Fox News to the 2021 attack on the Capitol:

> Fox News has helped to sell the fiction that the 2020 election was stolen from Trump, and there's a direct line from that lie to the rioting. There's a direct

line from that lie to various Republicans' attempts to develop mechanisms to overturn vote counts should they dislike the results.

In a recent article in the *New York Review of Books* Michael Tomasky (2022) adds Newsmax, One America News Network, *Breitbart News, The Blaze, The Federalist, The Daily Caller, The Washington Free Beacon,* right-wing talk-radio hosts, Christian radio and the Sinclair Broadcast Group (which pushes pro-Trump, right-wing views across the television and radio stations it owns in dozens of markets, and which received help in expanding its empire from Trump's Chairman of the Federal Communications Commission: McGill & Hendel, 2017). All of these outlets are agenda-driven in a way that the mainstream media are not. Their effectiveness is shown by the fact that, according to a CBS News/ YouGov poll, nearly 70% of Republicans do not think that Joe Biden is the legitimate winner of the 2020 election (Waldmeir, 2021).

Jacob Hacker (2011) attributed this growth in misinformation to the decline in intermediary organisations:

Middle-class democracy rested on organisations, such as unions and cross-class organisations, that gave middle class voters knowledge about what was at stake in policy debates as well as political leverage to influence those debates. Without this organisational grounding, voters simply have a very hard time drawing connections between what politicians do and the strains they face in their lives, much less formulating a broad idea of how those strains could be effectively addressed.[7]

In a personal communication, Bernard Abramson has drawn my attention to a recent (2021) paper by Martin Scheffer and colleagues that reports on an analysis of word use in millions of books in English and Spanish published between 1850 and 2019, alongside an analysis of *The New York Times* over the same period. In both sets of data, and for both fiction and non-fiction, they found (a) a shift from words associated with rationality (such as 'determine' or 'conclusion') to ones relating to human experience (such as 'feel' and 'believe'), and (b) a shift from a 'collectivistic' to an 'individualistic' focus (as reflected in the ratio of single to plural pronouns, such as 'I/we' and 'he/they'). In other words, there was a marked turn in language from rationality to emotion and from the collective to the individual. What is of particular interest in the present context is that both shifts occurred around 1980.[8]

The *Washington Post* (20 January 2021) famously estimated that in his four years, President Trump made 30,573 false or misleading claims. Peter Oborne's (2021) book details the stream of lies told by Boris Johnson when he was the *Telegraph's* man in Brussels, a trait that has continued under his Premiership (e.g., 'no border in the Irish Sea', 'all guidance [about lockdown parties] was followed completely in Number 10'). There can in fact be no better example than the February 2022 brouhaha that followed Johnson's statement by implication that when he was Director of Public Prosecutions, the Opposition Leader Sir Keir Starmer was personally responsible for the failure to prosecute the notorious paedophile Jimmy Savile (an assertion for which there was no factual basis and for which Johnson has refused to apologise, even at the cost of losing one of his longest and closest advisers).

Third, and perhaps most tellingly, both conservative parties have been very skilful in appealing to ordinary voters, exploiting the 'false consciousness' that was discussed in Chap. 5. Ideally, of course, the masses would be completely off the conservative political stage, but that is no longer realistic. To accommodate them, but retain control, Robin suggests that conservatives have typically adopted one of two main stratagems:

> *The masses must either be able to locate themselves symbolically in the ruling class or be provided with real opportunities to become faux aristocrats in the family, the factory, and the field. The former path makes for an upside-down populism, in which the lowest of the low see themselves projected in the highest of the high; the latter makes for a democratic feudalism, in which the husband or supervisor or white man plays the part of a lord.*
>
> *The former path was pioneered by Hobbes and Maistre, and the latter by Southern slaveholders, European imperialists and Gilded Age apologists. And neo-Gilded Age apologists. "There is no single elite in America", writes David Brooks. "Everyone can be an aristocrat within his own Olympus." Occasionally, as in the writing of Werner Sombart, the two paths converge: ordinary people get to see themselves in the ruling class by virtue of belonging to a great nation among nations, and they also get to govern lesser beings through the exercise of imperial rule.* (Robin, 2018: 30–31)

Another strategy is to portray elites as victims:

> *Encouraging the masses to see their abjection reflected in the higher misery of those above them. Regardless of the means, conservatism has always found a way to conscript the lower orders into its regime of lordly rule.* (Robin, 2018: 243)

It is indeed quite remarkable how successful politicians with moneyed backgrounds like Trump (a billionaire property developer who inherited $400 m from his father), Farage (a wealthy stockbroker) and Johnson (whose businessman father could afford to send him to Eton) have been in portraying themselves as victims of a nameless elite ('the swamp').

Overall, conservatives have been very effective in mobilising the masses in their support:

From revolutions, conservatives also develop a taste and talent for the masses, mobilizing the street for spectacular displays of power while making certain power is never truly shared or redistributed. That is the task of right-wing populism: to appeal to the mass without disrupting the power of elites or, more precisely, to harness the energy of the mass in order to reinforce or restore the power of elites. Far from being a recent innovation of the Christian Right, the Tea Party movement, or Trump, reactionary populism runs like a red thread throughout conservative discourse from the very beginning. (Robin, 2018: 52)

Finally, both conservative parties have been helped by the main progressive parties' turn away from their traditional values and sources of support (due partly to the changes brought in by the conservatives).

We noted in Chap. 4 that more than 20 years ago, the American sociologist Richard Rorty criticised the American Left for giving the Right the opportunity to exploit the impact of globalisation and downsizing on the labour market and many American households (Stuart Hall had uttered similar warnings in Britain). Similarly, Thomas Frank (2020) asserts:

It turns out that when the party of the left abandons its populist traditions for high-minded white-collar rectitude, the road is cleared for a particularly poisonous species of rightwing demagoguery. It is no coincidence that as Democrats pursue their professional class "Third Way", Republicans become ever bolder in their preposterous claim to be a "workers party", representing the aspirations of ordinary people.

In a December 2021 piece for *The New York Times* Jamelle Bouie asked:

What was the Democratic Party's response to a generation of neoliberal economic restructuring? What was its response to the near-total collapse of private-sector unions? What was its response to the declining fortunes of American workers and the upward redistribution of American wealth? (Bouie, 2021b)

Similar questions could be asked of the Blair Government in Britain: Peter Mandelson's 1998 comment about being 'intensely relaxed about the filthy rich as long as they pay their taxes' comes ineluctably to mind (Malik, S. 2012).

In Britain, Geoffrey Evans and James Tilley (2017) argued that as the numbers of the working class declined in the 1970s and 1980s because of changes in the structure of the economy enabled or reinforced by Neoliberal policies, both the major political parties switched their focus to the middle class. In response, the still substantial working class—now much more often deployed in service than manufacturing jobs—opted out of voting or even participating in politics altogether, at least until they had a new party that was closer to their views on EU integration or immigration and, even better, had an opportunity to express their views directly (as in the Brexit referendum). It is of course much easier in a first-past-the-post system than under proportional representation to ignore significant minorities like the shrinking working class.

In both countries, the centre-left parties have failed to show how much of the populist animus against the establishment is actually due to the conservative policies of tax cutting, restraining public expenditure and deregulation, the effects of which are then (almost incredibly) exploited by conservative (and even elite) politicians (Hacker, 2015). Nor have the progressives been able to exploit the fundamental lack of a common economic interest between the wealthy elites and the mass of popular support. This again reflects their turn towards cultural values, where the Left can never outperform the Right (however many Union Jacks Sir Keir Starmer chooses to picture himself with).

So it is not difficult to conclude that what we have been experiencing in both Britain and America since the late 1970s has been a conservative reaction to the long period of 'embedded Keynesianism' (Ruggie, 1982) from the 1930s to the 1970s. This is a conservative counter-revolution, of the kind anatomised by Robin, which has caused great social, economic, political and now environmental damage with very few compensating benefits. But can we just go back to before the late-1970s? How could we mount a progressive counter-counter-revolution?

7.1   A PROGRESSIVE COUNTER-COUNTER-REVOLUTION?

Four things would appear to be necessary if the conservative counter-revolution is to be rolled back:

1. The motives, effects and beneficiaries of conservative Neoliberal policies need to be called out.
2. The progressive parties need to work together in a systematic, organised fashion.
3. There have to be major reforms to the political system.
4. There needs to be a serious and sustained downward redistribution of resources and status.[9]

7.1.1   Calling out the Conservatives

First, we need to use all the (copious) evidence we now have to show how so many of our current social, educational, environmental, economic and political problems are due to, or have at least been exacerbated by, the beliefs and policies associated with Neoliberalism and the conservative counter-revolution. Of course, evidence on its own will not be sufficient. We have to emulate skilled practitioners like Reagan, Thatcher, Trump and Johnson and craft stories and slogans that will undercut the false narratives—'crowding out', the Laffer Curve, 'trickle-down' economics, 'the nation's economy is just like a household economy', the poor are welfare scroungers, 'anyone can work themselves out of poverty', etc.—that have led many people to see marketisation and deregulation as 'applied common sense' and Government and the state as public enemy number one (Aldred, 2019; Hope & Limberg, 2020).[10]

Substantively, we have to show that the route back to higher growth demands not tax or spending cuts but targeted state intervention and higher wages: workers who are paid more can spend more. We also have to resist the obfuscation that tries to explain disadvantage in cultural terms—'broken families', 'bad parents', 'damaged children', etc.—when the fundamental problem is material difference and insecurity (Wilkinson & Pickett, 2010).

The Covid crisis could help here. By virtue of the fact that it has been the poorer members of society who have been most damaged by it, the virus has shone a clear light on inequality and its effects (Hall & Taylor, 2020; Marmot, 2020; Romei, 2020; Deaton, 2021; Blundell et al., 2022). It is also showing the middle classes how meagre our levels of social protection (e.g., statutory sick pay) are, at least by European standards. It has stimulated interest in a universal basic income (Aldrick, 2020; Lansley, 2022). It cannot be a coincidence that the Neoliberal UK and US are amongst the high-income countries with the worst record of dealing with Covid (at least in the crucial early stages).

In February 2022, the House of Commons Public Accounts Committee estimated that fraud and error across all Covid-19 response measures totalled at least £15bn (Committee for Public Accounts 2022). This may become clearer when we have the report of Baroness Hallett's inquiry into the Johnson Government's handling of the pandemic. In the meantime, Hilary Cooper and Simon Szreter's (2021) analysis indicates that many of the by-now-familiar Neoliberal pathologies were present in the British Government's approach: giving economic considerations priority over social ones; a lack of response capacity due to austerity; a distrust of experts (in spite of claims to be 'following the science'); an insistence on centralised control; the outsourcing of key functions like 'test and trace' to inexperienced and inefficient private corporations when there were existing local public bodies that could do the job far better (and did so, when they were allowed to); the ministerial steering of lucrative PPE contracts to friends via a special VIP 'fast lane' (Casalicchio, 2021); huge profiteering as public procurers were taken for a ride by unscrupulous contractors (according to the Department for Health and Social Care's accounts, almost £10bn was spent on defective, unsuitable and overpriced personal protective equipment: Neville, 2022); and, last but not least, huge amounts of fraud, with the Treasury (almost unbelievably) writing off £4.3bn of the £5.8bn that was stolen from emergency schemes like furloughing, and which led to the resignation of the Minister for Efficiency and Transformation (Agnew, 2022).

Per contra, almost the only bright spot—the vaccination scheme—was due to sustained public investment in university research. In America, it appears that a major problem was inefficiency and lack of coordination by the major Federal agencies, possibly reflecting (at least in part) their past degradation (Stacey, 2022).

The crisis might even prompt the long overdue rethink about the way in which our societies and economies are run, as several respected commentators have suggested (e.g., Wolf, 2019; Elliott, 2020; Mazzucato, 2020a, 2020b; Goldin, 2021; Hennessy, 2022).

But there is also an argument that just because Covid-19—like the Coalition Government's response to the 2008 economic crisis (Wren-Lewis, 2018)—will bear most heavily on the low-paid, unskilled and those in insecure jobs, this will just reinforce populism and mistrust of Government (Stephens, P. 2020). In America, the Federal Government's initial failure to lead and coordinate a collective response to Covid (Politi et al., 2020) will have done little to make people warm to Government (at least at the Federal level).

However a very recent survey of individuals in 27 countries by the University of Cambridge Centre for the Future of Democracy finds evidence that the pandemic may be reversing the tide of populism (whether measured using support for populist parties, approval of populist leaders or agreement with populist attitudes). Unfortunately, however, they also find 'a disturbing erosion of support for core democratic beliefs and principles, including less liberal attitudes with respect to basic civil rights and liberties and weaker preference for democratic government' (Cambridge Centre for the Future of Democracy, 2022: 1).[11]

7.1.2   Progressives Working Together

Calling out the conservatives as a way of undermining the dominant position that conservative parties and groups have established politically over the past 40 or so years would be easier if the progressive parties were to pool their resources and work together more closely. In the US this would mean the two wings of the Democratic Party sticking together and suppressing their differences (especially when the Republican Party's cohesion, or at least that of its lawmakers, has been damaged by Trump). In Britain, it could mean some sort of progressive alliance between Labour, LibDems, Greens and Nationalists, perhaps beginning by agreeing to nominate only one anti-conservative candidate in each constituency at the next election: 'stand aside'.[12]

7.1.3   Reforming the Political System

In both Britain and America, the progressive forces would be united not only in calling out conservative policies but also in reforming our political systems so that they take far better account of the full range of groups and interests across our societies, and not just those with money and influence. This means ensuring that everyone who is entitled to vote is actually able to do so;[13] introducing some form of proportional representation to prevent large numbers of voters from being disenfranchised for living in the wrong place;[14] placing strict limits on, and ensuring full transparency of, the private funding of political parties and groups;[15] and exercising much tighter control over the statements and claims made in political communications in any medium.[16]

7.1.4   Reversing Upward Distribution

Finally, we need to advocate and adopt policies that will reverse the upward redistribution of resources and power over the past 40 years. This means not only reallocation through the tax and benefits system but also what has been called 'pre-distribution'. This in turn requires reforms to the labour market to adjust the balance of power between employers and workers (highlighted by P&O Ferries's instant dismissal of several hundred ferry crew in March 2022), as well as a serious crackdown on tax avoidance and corporate welfare through tighter market regulation and stronger anti-fraud resources and powers. More generally, every new Government policy should be tested for its impact on inequality, with the benefits and costs to equity fully assessed: 'inequality proofing'.[17]

In the US, President Biden has made a start with his Covid recovery bill, an infrastructure bill, and what has become known as Build Back Better for investment in human infrastructure. As David Brooks pointed out in *The New York Times* in November 2021, these will all funnel money to less educated, less affluent, 'left behind' areas. This may explain why they have been so strongly opposed not only by the Republicans but even by two Democrat Senators. In the UK, few independent observers think that the February 2022 White Paper (Department for Levelling Up, Housing and Communities, 2022) will bring about a serious regional redistribution, especially when so many current Government policies work in the opposite direction (for a more sympathetic analysis, see Wolf, 2022).

President Biden has also made a start in cracking down on kleptocracy: corruption, transnational money laundering and similar practices (White House, 2021). As several commentators have pointed out (e.g., Michel, 2022), this further exposes the failure of successive British Governments to tackle these and similar practices. It is only because of US pressure and the Ukraine crisis that the Government has finally brought forward legislation—the Economic Crime Bill—to create a register of overseas entities highlighting the ultimate owners of overseas companies that control property and land in the UK (Pickard, 2022). And even when the legislation is enacted, it is not clear whether it will be properly enforced (Grylls & Smyth, 2022; Sikka, 2022).[18]

Because of the way in which right of centre parties have captured and exploited our political systems, and have been increasingly driven by extremists, both Britain and America are now largely run by 'a minority of a minority' in the interests, very largely, of a small set of wealthy people, sectors and organisations: an oligarchy, although that term is rarely used. Unless and until this power imbalance is corrected, it is very hard to see how either country can seriously hope for a brighter, fairer and more productive future.

7.2   CONCLUSION

In an article in *The Guardian* in 2010, the noted historian of postwar Britain, David Kynaston, identified the conditions that had enabled the success of the austerity programme in the 1940s: shared purpose, equity of sacrifice, hope and confidence in the political class. Whilst reserving judgement as to how successful the new Coalition Government might be in delivering renewed austerity, he concluded:

> *Although Goethe rightly warned against exaggerating the importance of our own times, the stakes feel high. We have a society accustomed to the pursuit of prosperity and individual gratification, often resentful of immigrants, and possessing a perilously skin-deep attachment to democracy. There may be real trouble ahead if our rulers get it wrong.*

Unfortunately, as a result of the subsequent austerity programme, on top of the Neoliberal reforms of the 1980s and 1990s (and the inability or unwillingness of subsequent centre-left governments to reverse them), and in spite of the Covid crisis, we are now (in mid-2022) even further away from these success conditions than we were in 2010.

NOTES

1. Sayer (2015), Monbiot (2016) and Lansley (2022) all provide relevant UK surveys.
2. Dionne (2016: 134) reports Senator Barry Goldwater as saying in 1996 that he would now be seen as a liberal Republican. In the UK, the parallel exclusion of moderates was symbolised by the September 2019 expulsion from the Conservative Party of 21 MPs who had opposed Boris Johnson's Brexit legislation. They included several Ministers, two former Chancellors and Winston Churchill's grandson.
3. Katica Roy (2020) provides a good summary of the various ways in which the ability to vote is being directly constrained in the US. According to the independent Brennan Center of Justice, 19 states passed at least 34 laws restricting access to voting in 2021, and as of January 2022, at least 13 bills

restricting access to voting had already been filed for this year (Blow, 2022). A 2020 paper by Vincent Mahler, based on a cross-national analysis of developed democracies, also finds an *indirect* relationship, with the rate of electoral turnout being positively related to the extent of Government redistribution. This is especially the case where the redistribution is accomplished through transfers that affect the lower part of the income spectrum.

4. For a similar analysis for the UK, see Freedland (2021). Two articles in *The New York Times* in December 2021 (Bernstein and Staszewski; Greenhouse) argue that Republican populism now dominates the Supreme Court. One area where President Trump *was* highly effective was in populating the Federal courts with conservative justices. According to the Pew Research Center (Gramlich, 2021), the President left office having appointed over 200 judges to the Federal bench, including as many powerful appeals court judges in four years as President Obama did in eight. Federal judges have lifetime tenure so the conservative influence in the courts will continue almost indefinitely. Hacker and Pierson (2020: 159) quote the Senate Majority Leader, Mitch McConnell, as saying in January 2019:

> *My goal is to do everything we can for as long as we can to transform the federal judiciary, because everything else we do is transitory.*

This strategy has now borne fruit in the Supreme Court's June 2022 decision, in Dobbs vs. Jackson Women's Health Organisation, to abolish the constitutional right to an abortion (Greenhouse 2022).

5. For updates, see Epstein and Corasaniti (2022a and 2022b). Paul Krugman (2021) even suggests that the vehemency of Republican opposition to Biden's election reflects their understanding of the importance of vote rigging as a means of securing and retaining power.

6. A January 2022 Washington Post-University of Maryland poll showed that 40% of Republicans felt it was 'justified' in some cases for citizens to take 'violent action against the Government' (Fedor, 2022).

7. A 2018 study (Geraci et al.) suggests that access to broadband internet has led to a significant drop in forms of offline interaction and civic engagement. We should also note William Davies's view (2020: 33) that this epistemic crisis reflects the Neoliberal politicisation of the social sciences, metrics and policy administration which 'means that the "facts" produced by official statistical agencies must now compete with other conflicting "facts"'.

8. The authors do not offer any theory about the reasons, but they do speculate that 'there could be a connection to tensions arising from neoliberal policies which were defended on rational arguments, while the economic fruits were reaped by an increasingly small fraction of societies' (Scheffer et al., 2021: 6).

9. Robert Putnam (2020) thinks that what is needed is an 'upswing' towards economic growth and social equity, as experienced between the two wars and the 1960s. Based on how America entered into the Progressive Age (after World War I), he identifies the following requirements: active citizenship; local, grassroots activism leading to, and needing, regional and national consolidation; astute political entrepreneurs (like Teddy Roosevelt and Woodrow Wilson, and later FDR); and the mobilisation of youth.

10. In an admiring, even fawning, *Atlantic* profile of Johnson, Tim McTague (2021) writes:

> *To him, the point of politics—and life—is not to squabble over facts; it's to offer people a story they can believe in.*

11. Francis Fukuyama (2022) has suggested that the Russian invasion of Ukraine has done huge damage to populist leaders who previously expressed sympathy for President Putin (Matteo Salvini, Jair Bolsonaro, Eric Zemmour, Marine Le Pen, Viktor Orban and Donald Trump).

12. Barnett and Lawson (2020) identify 48 conservative seats where the combined 'progressive' vote surpassed the Tory total in 2019, enough to deprive the present Government of its Commons majority. At the 2021 Labour Conference, delegates representing the Party's membership voted 4 to 1 in favour of PR. Informal cooperation between Labour and the LibDems undoubtedly contributed to the 2021 Conservative by-election losses in Chesham and Amersham and North Staffordshire, as well as Labour holding on to Batley and Spen. There are now press reports (e.g., Parker & Cameron-Chileshe, 2022) that Labour will fight only a minimal campaign in the Liberal Democrats' top 30 target seats at the next general election. A November 2021 analysis by Best for Britain found that if the progressive parties were to field a single candidate in only a quarter of English parliamentary constituencies, this would be sufficient to remove the Government's majority. A September 2021 poll under the aegis of Make Votes Matter found a majority of voters in favour of PR, including voters from each of the major parties. Yet under the Elections Act 2022 the Government has removed the remaining Proportional Representation systems where they previously existed, in mayoral elections and police and crime commissioner elections (Behr, 2021).

13. Legislation introduced by the Democrats to counter the new voting restrictions and change the filibuster rules to enable it to pass was lost in the Senate in January 2022 (Hulse, 2022).

14. According to the Electoral Reform Society (Garland et al., 2020), in the 2019 general election over 22 m votes were ignored (70.8% of the total) because they went to unelected candidates or were surplus to what the elected candidate needed to win. In the US, the over-representation of

rural areas and the under-representation of urban areas is well-established (e.g., Silver, 2020).

15. Ideally, our political parties should be funded through a mixture of public and personal funds, with strict limits and full transparency (Foges, 2022). The close links between the very wealthy and the Conservative Government have recently been highlighted by a press investigation of a secret advisory board of major donors with direct access to Ministers (Pogrund & Zeffman, 2022). Questions have also been asked about the donations that a number of wealthy Russians have made to the Conservative Party (Walker, 2022).

16. In the US, many of the misinformation problems stem from the elimination of the Fairness Doctrine by the Federal Communications Commission in 1987. The Doctrine required broadcast licence holders to present controversial issues of public importance and to do so in a way that was honest, equitable and balanced. All four Commissioners at the time had been appointed by Republican Presidents and subsequent Congressional efforts to reinstate the policy were thwarted by Presidents Reagan and George H.W. Bush. The ending of the policy—on the grounds that since the Doctrine was first promulgated there had been such an explosion in the media that there was little danger of any opinion being neglected—has enabled the mostly conservative media to lie and mislead with almost total impunity (Professor Vaneeta D'Andrea, personal communication). In Britain, there can be little doubt that much of the conservatives' hostility to the BBC noted in Chap. 6 stems from the Corporation's attempts to preserve a balance in line with its charter, not to mention the enhanced commercial opportunities for the conservatives' allies and supporters if the BBC is cut down to size. Simon Kuper argued in the *Financial Times* in January 2022 that one of the things holding European societies together was the fact that most people still get their news from state broadcasters.

17. If it was serious about 'levelling up', the Government could bring into force the socioeconomic duty in Sect. 7.1 of the Equality Act 2010:

> *When making decisions of a strategic nature about how to exercise [their] functions, [public authorities must] have due regard to the desirability of exercising them in a way that is designed to reduce the inequalities of outcome which result from socioeconomic disadvantage.*

It could also reinstate the Cabinet Office Equalities Unit (abolished by the Coalition Government in 2010) to monitor and report on the implementation and effectiveness of the legislation and to propose any necessary changes.

18. A recently published book *Butler to the World: How Britain Became the Servant of Tycoons, Tax Dodgers, Kleptocrats and Criminals* by Oliver Bullough (Profile Books) shows how 'the unmatched financial and legal infrastructure that had allowed the UK to conquer a quarter of the world

was quietly repurposed to do the bidding of individuals from dubious regimes that it had sometimes fostered, and others who had seized control of their nation's resources and needed a place to hide what they had creamed off", to quote the *Observer* review (Adams, T. 2022).

REFERENCES

Adams, T. (2022, March 20). Bent Britain at your service. *The Observer.*

Agnew, T. (2022, January 24). Fraud is rampant – and no one in government is paying attention. *Financial Times.* Retrieved January 24, 2021, from https://www.ft.com/content/e7973f2e-32c2-4cab-9b12-13add89f8891

Aldred, J. (2019, June 6). The evils of bad economics. *The Guardian Journal.*

Aldrick, P. (2020, June 2). Coronavirus has united left and right on value of universal basic income. *The Times.*

Ballard, C. (2017) The fall and rise of income inequality in the United States: Economic trends and political-economy explanations. In: *Paper for a Conference at Michigan State University*, October 8–15, 2015.

Barnett, G., & Lawson, N. (2020). *We divide, they conquer: If Labour struggles to win alone, what is to be done?* Compass.

Behr, R. (2021, September 8). Tory MPs call it reform. But this elections bill looks like a heist. *The Guardian Opinion.*

Blow, C. M. (2022, March 14). Seven steps to destroy a democracy. *The New York Times.*

Blundell, R., Costa Dias, M., Cribb, J., Joyce, R., Waters, T., Wernham, T., & Xu, X. (2022). *Inequality and the Covid crisis in the United Kingdom.* Institute for Fiscal Studies Working Paper 22/01. Institute for Fiscal Studies.

Bouie, J. (2021a, December 3). The Trump conspiracy is hiding in plain sight. *The New York Times.* https://www.nytimes.com/2021/12/03/opinion/trump-bannon-2024.html.

Bouie, J. (2021b, December 10). So you lost the election. We had nothing to do with it. *The New York Times.* https://www.nytimes.com/2021/12/10/opinion/democrats-progressives-moderates-elections.html.

Bowcott, O., & Jones. S. (2008, January 23). Johnson's 'piccaninnies' apology. *The Guardian.*

Bruni, F. (2021, December 16). The line from Fox News to Trump's big lie is short and direct. *The New York Times.* Retrieved December 16, 2021, from https://www.nytimes.com/2021/12/16/opinion/fox-news-trump-january-6.html.

Cambridge Centre for the Future of Democracy. (2022). *The great reset: Public opinion, populism and the pandemic.* University of Cambridge Centre for the Future of Democracy.

Casalicchio, E. (2021, November 16). *Ex-Conservative Chair helped multiple firms to get UK PPE contracts*. Retrieved January 28, 2022, from https://www.politico.eu/article/conservative-uk-ppe-contracts-feldman-audit/.

Chaffin, J. (2021, January 19). 'He's kind of an ink blot': how the far-right fell in line behind Donald Trump. *Financial Times*. https://www.ft.com/content/6da53be7-e809-48d2-99f6-0e1348e68391.

Chinoy, S. (2019, June 26). What happened to America's political center of gravity? *The New York Times*. Retrieved June 26, 2019, from https://www.nytimes.com/interactive/2019/06/26/opinion/sunday/republican-platform-far-right.html.

Clarke, C. P. (2021, June 22). A new era of far-right violence. *The New York Times*. Retrieved June 22, 2021, from https://www.nytimes.com/2021/01/22/opinion/domestic-terrorism-far-right-insurrection.html.

Cohen, N. (2020, December 13). How did Enoch Powell, a man with no shame, come to haunt our times? *The Observer*.

Cohen, N. (2021, December 19). The Tories call it electoral reform. Looks more like a bid to rig the system. *The Observer*.

Committee for Public Accounts. (2022, February 2). *COVID-19 Cost Tracker Update. Thirty-eighth Report of Session 2021–22*.

Cooper, H., & Szreter, S. (2021). *After the virus: Lessons from the past for a better future*. Cambridge University Press.

Corasaniti, N. (2022, January 7). Voting rights and the battle over elections: What to know. *The New York Times*. Retrieved January 7, 2022, from https://www.nytimes.com/article/voting-rights-tracker.html.

Davies, W. (2020). *This is not normal: The collapse of liberal Britain*. Verso.

Deaton, A. (2021, January 5). Covid shows how the state can address social inequality. *Financial Times*. Retrieved January 5, 2021, from https://www.ft.com/content/caa37763-9c71-4f8d-9c29-b16ccf53d780.

Department for Levelling Up, Housing and Communities. (2022). *Levelling up the United Kingdom*. Department for Levelling Up, Housing and Communities.

Dionne, E. J. (2016). *Why the Right went wrong: Conservatism from Goldwater to Trump and beyond*. Simon and Schuster.

Edsall, T. (2022, January 19). Why millions think it is Trump who cannot tell a lie. *The New York Times*. Retrieved January 19, 2022, from https://www.nytimes.com/2022/01/19/opinion/trump-big-lie.html

Elliott, L. (2020, March 29). This crisis may force the world to rethink its economic models. *The Guardian*.

Epstein, R. J., & Corasaniti, N. (2022a, March 17). Republicans push crackdown on crime wave that doesn't exist: Voter Fraud. *The New York Times*.

Epstein, R. J., & Corasaniti N. (2022b, February 6). Taking the voters out of the equation: How the parties are killing competition. *The New York Times*.

Evans, G., & Tilley, J. (2017). *The new politics of class: The political exclusion of the British working class.* Oxford University Press.

Fedor, L. (2022, January 6) How Democrats failed to galvanise voters in year since January 6 riots. *The New York Times.*

Foges, C. (2022, March 7). Time to take sleaze out of political donations. *The Times.*

Frank, T. (2004). *What's the matter with Kansas? How Conservatives won the heart of America.* Picador.

Frank, T. (2020, November 9). Now Biden must tackle the causes of Trumpism. *The Guardian Journal.*

Freedland, J. (2021, October 2). The Tories are openly rigging the system to stay in power. *The Guardian Opinion.*

Fukuyama, F. (2022, March 10). Preparing for defeat. *American Purpose.* Retrieved March 15, 2022, from https://www.americanpurpose.com/articles/preparing-for-defeat.

Garland, J., Palese, M., & Simpson, I. (2020). *Voters left voiceless The 2019 General Election.* The Electoral Reform Society.

Geraci, A., Nardotto, M., Reggiami, T., & Sabatini, F. (2018). *Broadband internet and social capital.* Retrieved March 3, 2022, from iza.org/publications/dp/11855/broadband-internet-and-social-capital.

Goldin, I. (2021). *Rescue: From global crisis to a better world.* Sceptre.

Gramlich, J. (2021, January 13). *How Trump compares with other recent presidents in appointing federal judges.* Pew Research Center.

Greenhouse, L. (2022, June 24). Requiem for the Supreme Court. *The New York Times.* Retrieved June 24, 2022, from https://www.nytimes.com/2022/06/24/opinion/roe-v-wade-dobbs-decision.html.

Grylls, G., & Smyth, C. (2022, March 3). Budget cuts leave corruption investigators 'massively outgunned' by oligarchs. *The Times.* Retrieved March 3, 2022, from https://www.thetimes.co.uk/article/budget-cuts-leave-corruption-investigators-massively-outgunned-by-oligarchs-kmv5jlgdk.

Hacker, J. S. (2011). The institutional foundations of middle-class democracy. *Policy Network, 6,* 33–37.

Hacker, J. S. (2015, April 20). No cost for extremism: Why the GOP hasn't (yet) paid for its march to the right. *The American Prospect* Retrieved March 3, 2022, from prospect.org/cost-extremism.

Hacker, J. S., & Pierson, P. (2020). *Let Them eat tweets: How the right rules in an age of extreme inequality.* Liveright.

Hall, P., & Taylor, R. (2020, June 22). Pandemic deepens social and political cleavages. *Social Europe.* Retrieved February 1, 2021, from https://www.socialeurope.eu/pandemic-deepens-social-and-political-cleavages.

Hayter, B. (2022, February 8). *Government must ensure post-Brexit trade agreements receive parliamentary scrutiny.* Retrieved February 8, 2022, from https://www.politicshome.com/thehouse/article/goverment-must-ensure-postbrexit-trade-agreements-receive-proper-parliamentary-scrutiny.

Hennessy, P. (2022). *A duty of care. Britain before and after Covid.* Allen Lane.

Hope, D., & Limberg, J. (2020). *The economic consequences of major tax cuts for the rich.* International Inequalities Institute, London School of Economics Working Paper 55.

House of Commons Library. (2020). *UK election statistics: 1918–2019: A century of elections.* Briefing Paper CBP7529.

Hulse, C. (2022, January 19). After a day of debate, the voting rights bill is blocked in the Senate. *The New York Times.*

Kanno-Youngs, Z., & Sanger, D. E. (2021, January 27). Extremists emboldened by Capitol attack pose rising threat, Homeland Security says. *The New York Times.* Retrieved January 28, 2021, from https://www.nytimes.com/2021/01/27/us/politics/homeland-security-threat.html.

Kornhauser, W. (1959). *The politics of mass society.* Free Press.

Krugman, P. (2021, January 11). This putsch was decades in the making. *The New York Times.* Retrieved January 11, 2021, from https://www.nytimes.com/2021/01/11/opinion/republicans-democracy.html.

Kuttner, R. (2018). *Can democracy survive global capitalism?* W.W.Norton.

Lansley, S. (2022). *The richer, the poorer: How Britain enriched the few and failed the poor.* Policy Press.

MacLean, N. (2017). *Democracy in chains: The deep history of the radical right's stealth plan for America.* Scribe.

Malik, S. (2012, January 26). Peter Mandelson gets nervous about people getting 'filthy rich'. *The Guardian.*

Malik, N. (2020, August 31). The right's culture war is no sideshow. It's our politics now. *The Guardian Opinion.*

Marmot, M. (2020, December 15). Covid exposed inequality that must never be 'normal' again. *The Guardian Journal.*

Mazzucato, M. (2020a, March 18). The Covid-19 crisis is a chance to do capitalism differently. *The Guardian.* Retrieved March 19, 2020, from https://www.theguardian.com/commentisfree/2020/mar/18/the-covid-crisis-is-a-chance-to-do-capitalism-differently.

Mazzucato, M. (2020b, December 29). Covid exposes capitalism's flaws. *Financial Times.* Retrieved December 29, 2020, from https://www.ft.com/content/9e7b2630-2f67-4923-aa76-0f240a80a9b3.

McGill, M. H., & Hendel, J. (2017, June 8). How Trump's FCC aided Sinclair's expansion. *Politico.* Retrieved February 1, 2022, from https://www.politico.com/story/2017/08/06/trump-fcc-sinclair-broadcast-expansion-241337.

McTague, T. (2021). The Minister of Chaos: Boris Johnson knows exactly what he's doing. *The Atlantic.* Retrieved February 7, 2022, from https://www.theatlantic.com/magazine/archive/2021/07/boris-johnson-minister-of-chaos/619010/.

Michel, C. (2022, February 8). Tough US actions challenge Britain to step up the fight against kleptocracy. *Financial Times.* Retrieved February 9, 2022, from https://www.ft.com/content/09ba6575-a34a-4060-91b7-1885c9c720fe.

Monbiot, G. (2016). *How did we get into this mess?* Verso.

Monbiot, G. (2020, November 25). There is a civil war in capitalism and we're the collateral damage. *The Guardian Journal.*

Neville, S. (2022, February 1). UK squanders £10bn on defective or unsuitable PPE during pandemic. *Financial Times.*

Norton, P., & Aughey, A. (1981). *Conservatives and conservatism.* Temple Smith.

Oborne, P. (2021). *The assault on truth: Boris Johnson, Donald Trump and the emergence of a new moral barbarism.* Simon and Schuster.

Parker, G., & Cameron-Chileshe, J. (2022, February 17). Labour and Liberal Democrats in informal 'non-aggression' pact ahead of next election. *Financial Times.* Retrieved February 17, 2022, from https://www.ft.com/content/7d10aef7-1ed5-4e0d-a128-858cd0b2e2f0.

Pickard, J. (2022, February 28). Government brings forward bill to tackle UK's 'dirty money'. *Financial Times.* Retrieved March 2, 2022, from https://www.ft.com/content/b0bda4c4-def4-4816-9563-febba4834f28.

Pogrund, G., & Zeffman, H. (2022, February 19). The Tory donors with access to Boris Johnson's top team. *The Sunday Times.*

Politi, J., Fontanella-Khan, J., & Aliaj, O. (2020, June 18). Why the US pandemic response risks widening the economic divide. *Financial Times.* https://www.ft.com/content/d211f044-ecf9-4531-91aa-b6f7815a98e3.

Putnam, R. (with Garrett, S. R.) (2020). *The upswing: How we came together a century ago and how we can do it again.* Swift Press.

Robin, C. (2018). *The reactionary mind: Conservatism from Edmund Burke to Donald Trump* (2nd ed.). Oxford University Press.

Romei, V. (2020, December 31). How the pandemic is worsening inequality. *Financial Times.* https://www.ft.com/content/cd075d91-fafa-47c8-a295-85bbd7a36b50.

Rondeaux. C., & Hurlburt, H. (2021, January 25). How Parler reveals the alarming trajectory of political violence. *The New York Times.* https://www.nytimes.com/2021/01/25/opinion/parler-social-media.html.

Roy, K. (2020, September 29). America must end its shameful voter suppression. *Financial Times.* http://www.ft.com/content/fb1f8bc8-864b-45a1-91c5-8643e07a31dc.

Ruggie, J. (1982). International regimes, transactions, and change: Embedded Liberalism in the postwar economic order. *International Organization, 36,* 379–415.

Runciman, D. (2019). *How democracy ends.* Profile.

Rutter, J. (2019, December 27). How Brexit has battered our reputation for government. *The Guardian Journal.*

Sachs, J. D. (2021, January 8). *The truth about Trump's mob project syndicate.* https://www.project-syndicate.org/commentary/trump-mob-capitol-familiar-scene-of-white-mob-violence-by-jeffrey-d-sachs-2021-01.

Sample, I. (2021, December 31). UK government's Covid advisers enduring 'tidal waves of abuse'. *The Guardian.*https://www.theguardian.com/world/2021/dec/31/uk-governments-covid-advisers-enduring-tidal-waves-of-abuse.

Sayer, A. (2015). *Why we can't afford the rich.* Policy Press.

Scheffer, M., Leemput, I., Weinans, E., & Bollen, J. (2021). *The rise and fall of rationality in language.* https://doi.org/10.1073/pnas.2107848118. Accessed 10 January 2021.

Sikka, P. (2022, March 11). Why the Economic Crime Bill is unlikely to make a difference in stopping the flow of dirty money. *Left Foot Forward.* Retrieved March 14, 2022, from https://leftfootforward.org/2022/03/why-the-economic-crime-bill-is-unlikely-to-make-a-difference-in-stopping-the-flow-of-dirty-money/.

Silver, N. (2020, September 20). The Senate's rural skew makes it very hard for Democrats to win the Supreme Court. *FiveThirtyEight.* Retrieved November 6, 2020, from https://fivethirtyeight.com/features/the-senates-rural-skew-makes-it-very-hard-for-democrats-to-win-the-supreme-court.

Slobodian, Q. (2019, November 11). The defenders of 'economic freedom' fear democracy. *The Guardian Journal.*

Stacey, K. (2022, January 26). How the Biden administration failed the Omicron test. *Financial Times.* Retrieved January 26, 2022, from https://www.ft.com/content/449abc76-2cb4-4abf-a917-bcabf051cb7f.

Starr, P. (2019). *Entrenchment: Wealth, power, and the constitution of democratic societies.* Yale University Press.

Stephens, B. (2020, December 14). Donald Trump and the damage done. *The New York Times.* Retrieved December 14, 2020, from https://www.nytimes.com/2020/12/14/opinion/donald-trump-presidency.html.

Stephens, P. (2020, December 11). Like the financial crisis, Covid is a gift to populists. *Financial Times.* Retrieved December 11, 2020, from https://www.ft.com/content/3746ef63-d48a-4fa8-9b8a-45bc7c83d219.

Swaine, J. (2017, January 23). Donald Trump's team defends 'alternative facts' after widespread protests. *The Guardian.* Retrieved May 25, 2021, from https://www.theguardian.co/us-news/2017/jan/22/donald-trump-kellyanne-conway-inauguration-alternative-facts.

Temin, P. (2017). *The vanishing class: Prejudice and power in a dual economy.* MIT Press.

Tomasky, M. (2022, February 10). Can he build back better? *The New York Review of Books.*

Waldmeir, P. (2021, January 19). Trump supporters stay loyal but wary. *Financial Times.* Retrieved January 19, 2021, from https://www.ft.com/content/491be5e0-d1ab-4b61-89b6-1e1e422dd990.

Walker, P. (2022, February 23) Analysis: The Tories and Russia. *The Guardian.*

Walker, P., Stewart, H., & Siddique, H. (2021, May 14). Warning Johnson's ID plan risks freezing out over 2 million voters. *The Guardian.*

White House. (2021). *United States strategy on countering corruption.* Retrieved February 9, 2022, from https://www.whitehouse.gov/wp-content/uploads/2021/12/United-States-Strategy-on-Countering-Corruption.pdf.

Wilkinson, R., & Pickett, K. (2010, January 29). A broken society, yes. But broken by Thatcher. *The Guardian.* Retrieved November 29, 2018, from https://www.theguardian.com/commentisfree/2010/jan/29/social-mobility-inequality-conservative-thatcher.

Wolf, M. (2019, December 4). How to reform today's rigged capitalism. *Financial Times.* Retrieved December 4, 2019, from https://www.ft.com/content/4cf2d6ee-14f5-11ea-8d73-6303645ac406.

Wolf, M. (2020, December 8). Milton Friedman was wrong on the corporation. *Financial Times.* Retrieved December 10, 2020, from https://ft.com/content/e969a756-922e-497b-8550-94bfb1302cdd.

Wolf, M. (2021, September 28). The strange death of American democracy. *Financial Times.* Retrieved January 24, 2022, from https://www.ft.com/content/a2e499d0-10f0-4fa2-8243-e23eedc4f9f4.

Wolf, M. (2022, February 6). The levelling-up white paper is a necessary call to arms. *Financial Times.* Retrieved February 7, 2022, from https://www.ft.com/content/19c28c15-cd88-40bs-bd7a-15115b624ef5.

Wren-Lewis, S. (2018). *The lies we were told: Politics, economics and Brexit.* Bristol University Press.

INDEX[1]

[1] Note: Page numbers followed by 'n' refer to notes.